Self-Employment – The Secret to Success

Essential Tips for Business Start-Ups

------------ ≈≈≈≈ ------------

I would like to dedicate this book to
my husband Jude Fernando,
my parents and my brother.

------------ ≈≈≈≈ ------------

Contact Information

I would highly appreciate and value your feedback and suggestions to continue to improve this book's usefulness. Therefore, please do not hesitate to email me constructive comments and honest feedback.

I look forward to hearing your views.

You may reach me via lalani32@yahoo.co.uk.

Enjoy!

------------ ≈≈≈≈ ------------

Picture Copyright

Unless otherwise stated, no picture or graphical image in this book may be used, copied, reformatted, reproduced and distributed for any purpose, without the written permission of the Author.

All Rights Reserved

This book or any part of this publication thereof maybe not reproduced or used, in any form or by any means whatsoever, without the written permission of the Author.

------------ ≈≈≈≈ ------------

NOTE: The material contained in this book is set out in good faith for general guidance and no liability can be accepted for loss or expense incurred as a result of relying on circumstances described and statements made in the book. The business laws and regulations are liable to change, and readers should check the current position with the relevant authorities before making personal arrangements to start out in business.

Self-Employment – The Secret to Success

Essential Tips for Business Start-Ups

The Beginner's Guide to Setting up and Managing a Small Business

Lalani Jay (MBA, BCS)

Acknowledgements

Firstly, I would like to extend my gratitude to my husband for his initial guidance of my efforts in writing this book and for sharing his views, experiences and knowledge for improvement. Also his suggestion to include pictures and diagrams in the book has certainly added real value and enhanced its usefulness and convenience for the reader. Jude, your patience, constant support and comments immensely helped me get through the final steps of this journey, and I am truly grateful to you for that.

Also, I would like to express my special thanks to my brother Shamil for sourcing the right people to do the artwork, illustrations, pictures and the cover design to make this read an attractive one.

Finally, I would like to express my gratitude to all those who provided support in numerous ways in completing this book.

Self - Employment – The Secret to Success

If you want to create a successful business doing something you love and be your own boss, or you have recently started a business and want to take it to the next level, then this book is especially for you.

As you are making the challenging decision to start your own business, knowing that the direction towards success will be a bumpy road, can be an overwhelming thought. If you know the rules, boundaries, limitations, your abilities and when to stop early, then it will save you from great losses and many pitfalls along the way.

Here's the book to give you some important secrets, tips and step-by-step guidance on how to get started and invaluable information for the initial stage of your small business journey.

This read is crammed with high quality content, previously tested information, business strategies, tips and concepts that introduce clarity and order into your business, when you need it the most.

This book will, in particular, help you to find out:

- Whether self-employment is for you
- How to set goals
- How to measure your social media and website success
- How to manage your business days

And answer questions such as:

- What does it mean to be your own boss?
- What if your business is new to the market?
- What if you are frustrated and feel like giving up?
- What pitfalls can you avoid while running your business?
- How can you create and expand your business?

This book is invaluable for every business owner who aspires to succeed.

So, as you are reading through this book, pluck up your courage to gear up for the venture ahead, because success is not too far away!

Enjoy this book and take the steps to change your life forever!

CONTENTS

Chapter – 1   **1**

  Is Self-Employment Right for You?   1

    Initial Steps to Success   2

    The Next Steps   8

    Skills and Qualifications   11

    Peple to Talk to Before You Start   14

Chapter – 2   **17**

  A Guide to Writing a Business Plan   17

    Benefits of a Business Plan   18

    What Should Be Included?   18

    Common Mistakes to Avoid in a Business Plan   29

Chapter – 3   **33**

  Starting - Up   33

    Getting Your Business Off the Ground   34

    Preparing for Business   44

    Seven Reasons Why New Businesses Fail   45

    Structuring Your Business   49

    Pitfalls to Avoid   51

Chapter – 4   **53**

  Running Your Business   53

    Setting Objectives   57

    Market Research   60

Staying Ahead	62
Buyer Behaviour	64
Importance of Promotion	67
Using Technology in Your Business	71
Up and Running	73
Monitoring Business Performance	75

Chapter – 5   79

Managing Cash Flow and Planning for Success	79
Financial Forecasts	81
Tips to Improve Your Cash Flow	84
Business Tax – The Basics	84
The Books You Must Keep	87
Growing Your Business	89
Health Check Your Business	91
Planning for Success	92

Chapter –6   99

Getting Ready for Marketing	99
Marketing Plan	100
Writing a Marketing Plan	101
Know Your Customers	104
Customer-led Marketing	107
Improving Customer Loyalty	109
Further into Marketing	113
Marketing vs. Advertising – The Difference	116

Chapter – 7 — 117

Advertising Your Business — 117

- The Secrets of Successful Advertising — 123
- Where Does Advertising Go Wrong? — 126
- Designing Your Advertisement — 127
- The Right Medium for Your Advertising — 128
- Style of Writing — 131
- Persuading the Customer — 133
- The Checklist — 134

Chapter – 8 — 137

Getting Your Business on the Web — 137

- A Professional Website is Essential — 139
- How to Make Your Website a Success — 140
- Seven Guidelines for Exceptional Website Design — 144
- Maintaining Your Website — 147

Chapter – 9 — 149

Basic Sales Techniques — 149

- Sales Interface — 151
- Customer-Oriented Selling — 152
- Types of Customers — 154
- Motivational Schemes — 155
- 10 Secrets of a Successful Salesperson — 156
- Negotiating a Sale — 159
- Selling Styles — 160

Chapter – 10   163

Using the Latest Technology in Your Business   163

- Information System Benefits   168
- Competitive Strategies   170
- Use of Project Management Software   171
- Activities Involved in a Project   172
- Why Do Projects Fail?   173
- Outsourcing   175

Preface

There's so much to think about when you are starting a business. Starting any type of business venture carries an element of risk and the whole process is a challenging one. However, starting your own business simply means doing what you enjoy doing the most. To run a business successfully will require you to spend long hours, do a lot of thinking and have many sleepless nights. So, it is very important to make sure starting your own business is what you really want to do. Self-employment is a lifestyle. It can give you a great deal of flexibility in terms of how and when you work. Ideally, you can set your own hours, your own rules and time frames, and decide what you do, how to do it and when you want to do it.

People choose to become self-employed for a variety of reasons, independence and flexibility being the primary ones. Being your own boss can potentially offer you a better work/life balance. It is also true that improved quality of life and increased job satisfaction are important aspects of going self-employed. However, the risk is that there can be a huge amount of responsibility involved, and a regular pay cheque at the end of the month cannot be guaranteed. Running a business has lots of responsibilities and pressures. Start-ups especially need to work a lot harder to establish themselves than those who are already in the market, until they are seen and heard well enough for the consumer to buy from them. Therefore, you need to work as hard as it takes to become known.

It is a risk to start the business until you are satisfied and confident that you have the right skills, the 'hunger' and the 'drive' to succeed. You must be ambitious and have a great desire for growth.

Launching a business is extremely tough if you don't have the time to devote to it. Also you need to establish whether there is a large enough market for the product or service you are planning to sell.

Additionally, a considerable amount of preliminary research will be necessary in order to find out who and where your competitors and potential customers are. Therefore you need to plan your time carefully.

Planning in advance will ensure that you will always know where you are and what direction you are heading in. You must also have specific goals that you are planning to achieve, within a set time period. It is important to constantly plan for success from the very beginning of your journey knowing that your efforts will be rewarded one day.

Business owners must have self-belief, a positive attitude, energy, resilience, and patience in abundance, to make the business work. No doubt, it is a lot of Hard Work! Starting a business can often take longer than you think. Take your time and get it right and it will be worth it. Do not ever give up when the going gets tough.

You're the BOSS and you make the decisions! Do it right, the first time!

Best of Luck!

« CHAPTER – 1 »

Is Self-Employment Right for You?

It is encouraging to see how many people dream of setting up their own business and becoming successful. Once you become a business owner, in a few years time you will be a different person. You will be: better organised, self-disciplined and more realistic.

However, becoming self-employed can bring its own stress. Nevertheless, most entrepreneurs never want to return to nine to five jobs, even if they fail.

The general statistics suggest one in five businesses fail in the first five years. Therefore, to become your own boss and run a successful business is a challenge in itself. The challenge is to be at least one step ahead of the others in the market if you are thinking of 'victory'.

Initial Steps to Success

First, you need to lay a solid foundation to build your business upon. Or else it will collapse sooner than you think.

Therefore, before you take up the challenge, it is important to check that you are ready to face up to it.

Initially your ride will not be as smooth as you think it will be, and you will have to face a lot of unforeseen obstacles along the way.

Start by taking the following initial steps, which are known to give the persuasive edge that a start-up business will certainly need.

1) A Good Business Plan

A good business plan is an essential tool for a start-up. Making sure you have a clear vision for your business and that you have noticed a gap in the market is important here. Also you must be certain that your business can deliver a distinct service or product than your competitors.

Preparing a good business plan will help you to define and bring into focus where you want your business to go and how you are going to get there. This business plan should fundamentally include a description of your business, information on your services or products, revenue projections, financial requirements and intended marketing methods.

An ideal business plan consists of three to ten pages that describe important information about your business and financial data. Excessive detail should be included in appendices. No one will want to read lengthy and complicated details, no matter how good the plan is.

It is important to set out what your business will become, what your market is, who your target customers are and what your competitors are doing.

Simultaneously, you should include details about how you are hoping to promote your business and where you are planning to be in five years time. Focusing on such information early on, will help you to become aware of the weaknesses, limitations, opportunities and strengths of the business.

Incorporating long-term objectives, forecasts and as many measurable goals as possible in your business plan, while justifying every assumption will also be very helpful. A steady plan will potentially secure investors when you need to raise additional funds to run your business in the long term.

You can also get advice from your local bank on how to create your business plan if you are in doubt. Or you may find further information you need by simply logging onto the Internet and carrying out basic research.

2) Assess Your Abilities and Resources

It is important to assess your abilities and resources before you start your business. Sheer determination, motivation, mental and physical energy are just some of the essential attributes a promising entrepreneur must have to begin this challenging business journey.

You may also want to consider what sort of person you are: Do you have good communication skills; are you a leader or manager who is creative and flexible, and are you able to plan and make decisions under pressure?

Extensive research needs to be carried out and you need to plan out the things you must do before you can get your business off the ground.

Therefore, ask yourself the following questions before you make the challenging decision to become self-employed:

    a) Do you have the necessary initial finance and resources for at least the first year?
    b) Do you have the commitment, determination and self-discipline to face potential hard times?

c) Are you confident in your negotiation skills?
d) Do you know what the demand is for your product or services?
e) Do you know when to stop, if something is not working?

Here, you need to be honest about your weaknesses and strengths and identify what you do best and what you do poorly before you even begin. Get advice from family, friends and experts to evaluate your own abilities.

Involve friends and family or get a professional to help you with areas where you are weak. Being honest and realistic about what you can and can't do, is a sign of true long-term success.

Stick to your strengths and distribute other tasks to people who have the skills to do the job.

Simultaneously, you must not forget to measure the tangible assets and resources you own at the start of your business to evaluate the capacity and competence that you may have over your competitors.

3) Research the Market

Find out more about what your market needs before implementing your business idea. Your market research should at least cover areas such as the size of the market, the demand for your products or services, the future, and information about your likely competitors. Make sure your product or service is a 'must-have', not an 'optional', in the market.

Once you have got a good business idea to sell a product or service, you need to know if your potential customers can see the need to want to buy it. Trying to sell a product or service that is new to the market can be an uphill struggle. Being the first in the market has its advantages, but is not always the best situation. As you launch a new product or service it is crucial to educate people and convince them of the need to buy it.

Making your promotional activities stand out and doing them differently will allow you to highlight features and benefits more effectively to impress potential consumers.

Selling a product or service that exists and adding better quality and value to it, will confirm a strong place for your business.

Therefore, doing what you do best and finding that 'gap' in the market is essential for success.

Know your market better than your competitors and carry out as much market research as you can, concentrating on current demand and changing needs.

Carrying out brain storming sessions with potential customers, distributors and suppliers is also beneficial for long term growth.

4) Importance of Trading Name

An easy to remember, creative business name is vital for any business. The 'Brand Name' plays a vital role in making people remember what you sell. Carry out some research and think up something catchy that will stick in people's heads, or something that will get people thinking.

Have some names printed BIG and **bold** and post them on the wall of a spare room or office room or bedroom or on a board that is clearly visible to you, so that you see them often.

Also when you select a name, don't forget to take ideas and opinion from your family members, friends, ex-colleagues and experts to establish its precision.

Think long and hard before you make your choice. And make that choice the 'right one'. Carry out checks to ensure that the name you have selected is available for you to use and that no one else is using the same name.

It is always ideal to come up with a unique name as possible, and something that expresses what your business is all about.

Once you have decided on 'The Name', authenticate the meaning of the name from the dictionary, just to make sure that what you have selected has the appropriate meaning.

Once you are completely happy with the name you have chosen, have it printed on all your stationery, business cards and all marketing material available to you.

And now it is time to make people aware!

5) Polish Up Your Permits

Before launching your business, it is necessary to check what the licence or permit requirements for your business are. In some industries it is required to hold certain qualification to trade, such as a qualification in Law, Accountancy, Medicine or a licence from your local authority, etc.

Also, if you are using software on your computers, do not forget to update those licences when necessary. There may be site licences that you need to consider getting as well. Consider what these requirements are, and do not ignore the licensing rules that may apply to your business.

If you are not sure whether your business needs a licence or permit to operate, then your local council will be able to offer you advice and guidance on the subject. Taking advice from your accountant or solicitor will also be helpful in this regard.

Keep company registration, tax registration and details of licences on file at a safe and secure location for reference at any given time. Getting your business as organised as possible will make your life easier, and doing so will improve your ability to focus, enabling you to reach your goals and fulfil your ambitions quicker.

6) Your Workspace

The place where your business is located is the key, if your sales are largely based on customer in-store visits.

This maybe applicable, when a potential consumer needs to see and feel the product he or she is considering buying, or when it is necessary to meet the people before signing up to a service.

It is important to look for a location where you can afford to set up, close to your customer base.

You will be particularly fortunate if you can set up your workspace at home in the initial stages of your small business journey, to cut down on costs. However, you may need to obtain particular permits from your local authority, if your clients need to visit your property to obtain services or products. If your customers are visiting your 'home' office, ensure the home environment is pleasant, quiet, clean and tidy.

Organise an attractive setting with fresh flower arrangements, make use of an air freshener and make sure it is presentable. Make your customers feel comfortable in your office.

Also, giving your customers clear guidance on public transport or car parking facilities prior to their visit will make them feel welcome! It is very important to create a good first impression, if you want to make a sale.

Meeting your first customers in a coffee shop or free or affordable meeting place is also feasible. Consider local businesses or friends who would be happy to share their office space with you, until you are able to open an office of your own. There are many flexible business offices with meeting facilities and someone to take your phone calls available nowadays, that will give you prominent business addresses in the city.

When your business becomes successful you may be able to choose the best location for your office in a city centre with close proximity to public transport, car park facilities and other amenities.

When you are taking these crucial steps as you start out, you must also think about taking your business five more steps forward, as described below.

The Next Steps

Many start-ups feel the pressure in today's evolving business environment. As a new business owner, you will often feel overwhelmed. You must always be confident and deliver what you promise to deliver, not forgetting to stress the benefits of your products or services to your customers. Expressing a positive image of your business at this early stage will make the most of your sales. In addition, this positive image will earn you loyal long-term customers who are one of the biggest assets for the growth of your company.

You need to view the following initiatives as long term growth accelerators.

1) Give Your Business the Persuasive Edge

Whatever type of business you own, you probably started it because you have the technical expertise, design flair, subject knowledge or just had a bright idea. Yet people won't come to you unless you tell them what you do loudly enough. You need to persuade people to buy from you by introducing the benefits of your products and services, as often as necessary.

However, be honest about what you can offer and never promise what you cannot deliver. Give your customers sufficient time to make that important 'buying decision'. Make every effort to answer all queries raised by a potential customer. Allow time for a productive conversation and highlight the good features of your products or services. Make your business stand out.

You need to be persuasive without being too aggressive to make a sale. Offer something more, different or better than your competitors.

2) Avoid a Vague Tone

It is in our nature that we lose interest when everything someone says begins with the word 'I'.

Try starting a conversation with the word 'you'. It will sound very thoughtful and that is the way your customers like it. Talk clearly, be honest, be respectful and pleasant during any conversation between you and your customer, at any time of the day.

3) Avoid Suspicion

Anything you discuss with customers must reflect your confidence. There is no place for 'I think', 'I hope', 'probably', 'maybe' or 'perhaps' within a successful conversation.

You need to include cutting-edge ideas and creative suggestions during any negotiation. Also, avoid weak description of your products or services at all times. You must know your 'goods' well to be able to sell them confidently.

Never describe a suggested feature as being quite interesting, but rather, use words that add originality or inspiration.

However, if you are not sure about anything related to the product or service, please do take advice from an expert or do research before answering any customer queries. It is useful to have a thorough knowledge about your business and what it sells. Only the companies that adapt to changes quickly enough will survive longer than the others.

4) Stress the Benefits

To increase the chances of a sale of your products or services, you should constantly emphasise their benefits. The distinguishing features should be well expressed. People increasingly look for benefits when they are serious about making a purchase. Also, listen to what they have to say. Use their constructive feedback for further improvement.

Remind your customers that, what you sell is worth buying for the price they will pay. Show testimonial of happy customers who have brought from you.

These testimonials must reflect the typical experiences of your genuine customers. Building a close connection with your potential customers is crucial.

5) Make Things Interesting

There should be a clear beginning, middle and end in the products or services that are being offered. What you say must reflect something attractive about your business. Make sure you sound friendly, efficient, professional, knowledgeable and reasonable. Ensure such characteristics show, when talking to your customers. Grab their attention with a powerful start, led by benefits, followed by features and you need to maintain that interest throughout.

Share interesting stories and experiences with your customer. This will definitely bring opportunities to progress to the next level.

One satisfied customer and strong relationship carry repeat sales.

∞

Most business owners who do well share a similar skills set. Therefore, you will need to understand these essential qualities that make them different and successful, and involve and use those skills for your own success.

If you are seriously focused on making your businesses work, then it is important to possess certain qualities and take on board some people skills to win new deals. However, bear in mind that you don't need to possess all of these skills or characteristics to run your business successfully.

But the key is to develop, grow and strengthen these skills as you go along. Knowing what these characteristics are and what they can do to build up your business and help you become successful, will be invaluable for any business owner.

Characteristics of a Successful Business Owner

Although some people have a natural talent for entrepreneurship, it doesn't mean that every individual who aspires to succeed does not have the skills and abilities to accomplish their dreams. However, before stepping into running your own business it is important to understand your talents, improve on them, and learn new skills to achieve your goals.

The company owners are the strength of any business and it is very important your business should suit your skills and personality.

Skills and Qualifications

Apart from the above characteristics, having some basic skills and qualifications will be an added advantage for any individual who is hoping to become self-employed.

1) Technical Skills

Customers will be more comfortable and convinced about buying from you if you have the appropriate knowledge about the products or services you sell, and if you have adequate technical skills to run your business successfully.

Knowing the basics may not be enough to obtain the licences you may require for a business to operate. For example, if you are running a small business in IT or Law, then it is necessary to have an IT or Law degree to carry out the tasks that are required of you. Alternatively, you can also employ an expert or a professional to carry out the required services for you if they are not core to your services. If it's a law firm, you will need to be qualified to practice.

2) Business Skills

Business skills are essential for a sole trader to manage and operate a business successfully. Ideally you should get some training on business administration and general activities well before launching any type of venture. Obtaining advice and help to sharpen your knowledge and refine awareness will be useful for long-term business growth.

3) Leadership Skills

If you expect your business to grow more rapidly, you need to have great leadership skills and a good ability to lead people in the right direction. Many businesses fail due to lack of strong leadership and effective decision-making skills of business owners. A good leader must be largely responsible for the success or failure of the business.

Great leaders share knowledge, take quality decisions, communicate effectively and lead by example, to achieve success. Leaders must 'lead' with their actions as well as their words. Good leaders put that 'extra 5%' into the business in whatever task they take on, to make a difference.

4) Selling Skills

As you begin to trade, it is necessary to persuade people to buy your products or services on an ongoing basis. But it is important not to be too aggressive or forceful about it, is important, or the potential buyers may want to stop using your goods or services. Learning good selling techniques will win you some potential long term customers, even from your biggest competitor. Being out-going, approachable and reliable are some essential qualities of a good salesperson. Customers may like your good attitude, simplicity and honesty. Never make your sales complicated or leave it to other people who are working with you to do the sale for you. Take the initiative and go with your best instincts.

5) Organisational Skills

In order for you to run your business effectively, you must be well organised, resourceful and up to date. Planning ahead, managing your time and finance carefully, and good discipline will take your business to higher levels.

Effective organisation of tasks and time will improve productivity in the company to a greater extent. It is not ideal to unnecessarily spend a lot of time performing a task or discussing a sale. Know where to draw the line. It is also important to keep records of phone calls and text messages within a system to follow-up your customers in the future. Organise all important documents in relevant files and folders and store them securely in your office. Early planning and systemising things appropriately will definitely increase the productivity and efficiency of your business activities.

People to Talk to Before You Start

Seeking expert advice on various aspects of your new venture is always important. Do not misjudge the value of investing in good professional guidance from people who are already in business. Learn from their experiences, gain invaluable knowledge and get the latest information about the market from them. It is essential to get the basics right and establish what you are planning to achieve, from very early on. Planning is important in order to ensure you start out correctly.

These people will be able to point you in the right direction give you advice and guidance and might even help you in the crucial decision-making process in your business.

Doing everything necessary to build awareness about various key areas in today's competitive business world is worthwhile.

Speak to people, learn from their experiences, get diverse views and opinion and evaluate how you can use this knowledge for the benefit of your business.

Talking to the individuals or organisations listed below will give you the confidence that you might desperately need to kick start your business:

a) Speak to your partner, family, friends, colleagues and current boss.
b) Speak to your local authority or council.
c) Do your research and speak to successful entrepreneurs.
d) Make use of professional networks, social media and business networks.
e) Spend time with your bank or potential investors.
f) Get advice from an accountant and a solicitor.

Remember, the information and experiences collected from these people will be extremely useful to you as the business begins to operate.

With this information in hand, you might be able to take necessary precaution and avoid potential hazards along the way.

∞

« *The Guideline* »

Always remember, the pressure of running a business is unavoidable. If things go wrong, no one will be responsible but you. You may even get into debt and have to cope without a regular income for some time. There will be times when you need to be strong, and there will be times when you feel like giving up, defeated and isolated. So you will need faith and constant reminders about your motives for becoming a business owner in the first place.

Also, there will be many difficult times when you need to be courteous and cooperative even if you don't feel like it, especially when dealing with an awkward customer.

The pressure on you will be unbearable at times and you need to be aware of these potential negative situations. Be alert and prepared to deal positively with the challenges that might come your way. It is time to develop your confidence and be optimistic to get through those bad times!

« CHAPTER – 2 »

A Guide to Writing a Business Plan

Writing a business plan is the first and one of the most important tasks that you must think about when starting a business. And you will need to carry out thorough research to find out if there is a market for your products and services. Once you have done your research, established proof that there is a gap in the market for what you are planning to offer, and you are certain about it and committed to proceeding, then, the next stage is to consider putting together a business plan. This initial plan will help you set targets, assemble your ideas and prepare your finances.

Once the initial plan is created, and the business is launched, the plan must be reviewed regularly, in order to identify the changes that may have occurred during operation. A good business plan sets up strategies to monitor performance of the business, helps you keep track of targets and assists you with ideas for improvement. Therefore, you need to spend a considerable amount of time on your business plan, for it to be as effective as possible.

Benefits of a Business Plan

Make sure your business plan clearly describes your business, that it is easy to read, and there are no inconsistencies in it. The plan needs to be realistic, and the business needs to be able to support you. A business plan is important, because it will explain two things that you should know before committing yourself to starting a business. Essentially they are: how much you will earn if things go well, and how much it could cost you if things don't go as planned.

Preparation of a business plan forces you to clarify the precise direction that you wish to take. If there are fundamental flaws in your plan, it will help you to discover these at the beginning. Also, a carefully thought-out business plan may assist you in raising additional finances to get your business off to a good start.

Here are some of the benefits a good business plan can bring to your business:

- Formulates research and inspires ideas
- Helps establish targets and objectives of business
- Assists with setting up marketing strategies
- Enables monitoring of business performance
- Predicts future dangers
- Guides preparation of safety measures and prevents from pitfalls

∞

What Should Be Included?

A business plan describes your business's future, and ideally it must tell you exactly what you want to achieve and how. Your business plan essentially helps you turn your idea into a reality.

A Well-Rounded Business Plan is Essential

Consider incorporating the above elements in your plan. And don't be put off; writing a business plan doesn't have to be hard.

1) Executive Summary

This is a brief summary of the plan, not more than two pages long.

You must include the following in the first part of the summary:

    a) Business name, owners details and business address
    b) Details of products and services

c) Your target market and competition
   d) Amount of investment made
   e) Amount of further finance required

Also, there are four key elements to your executive summary. They will be:

   f) What makes your product or service unique
   g) What experience you and your team have in your target market
   h) How your business will be viable and profitable
   i) How and when the investors will get their money back

2) Aims, Objectives and Vision

For many people, the objectives of starting up a business are the degree of independence, and the ability to earn a reasonable income, and a decent life-style. Therefore, you must focus on building your business quickly and visualise where you want your business to be in five years. The vision statement of your business will help to guide you towards your goals so you can achieve them effectively, while avoiding threats and pitfalls.

3) Business Background, History and Purpose

This includes a good description of exactly what the business will be doing and details of products and services you are planning to offer. It is important to outline what the product and services will do for the customer and what differentiates your products and services from those already available in the market.

If yours is a new business, then you must describe what the business is all about, and the details of the owner's background and experience. If your business is already up and running, this section must explain when the business was started, how it has developed and details of any significant milestones or achievements.

Writing a mission statement here, will also clearly summarise the purpose of your business.

4) The Projects

If you are planning to expand the business in the future, it is recommended to add new products, services, ideas and create a project plan for further development. Reasons behind the project initiation, the benefits they will bring to the business, cost savings and capital expenditure should be outlined, here. Additionally, setting out the funding required, and its intended use, must be explained in detail in this section.

5) Legal Status and Licences

This section is to detail the status of your company such as whether you are a sole trader, in partnership or a limited company or another type. Depending on the status of your business, you must decide when you will pay tax and identify how that will affect your cash flow. As previously stated find out if your business is required to obtain any licences before it begins trading. If you work from home, you may need to obtain permission from your landlord or building society or council to be able to trade.

6) Management Structure, Staffing and the Process

Make an assessment of the key skill set that you and your team members hold, the responsibilities each one can take, and the jobs each member can perform to the best of their ability.

Evaluate the work needs to be carried out on key areas of your business, which you might need to manage effectively, and allocate the right people to, such as:

- Administration
- Finance
- General Management
- Product/Service Development
- Sales and Marketing
- Technology Support

A full background profile for every member of staff and the management team must be outlined.

It is fundamental to demonstrate here, the experience and talent each team member can bring to the business to provide an excellent service or product. Ideally, a projection of required levels of staff over the next three years should also be described.

Additionally, the work that must be done to recruit these people and the minimum skills required to run the business at a satisfactory level will be summarised in this section.

7) Training Needs

This is the space to include details of any training courses you have had and any training needs you may have in your business plan for further development. What could also go here are the budget for training costs and other needs to accelerate growth.

8) Premises and Equipment

Details of the present premises in terms of freehold, leasehold or rented status with details of monthly or annual payments must be included on this part of the plan. Also, information about capital expenditure for all equipment purchased for a minimum of three years, reasons for such purchases, and how new equipment will bring cost savings and operational efficiency, must be explained here too.

9) Market Situation

Research the size of the market and current trends. Study the market situation and understand your potential customers. Think about the benefits that your customers are looking for, and what your products and services are offering theirs. List your competitors and describe how your products and services will be different from them. You need to have a clear understanding of your target market and describe the market situation.

10) Marketing Analysis and Strategy

It is easier to define your marketing strategy, if you have clearly identified the market size, location, potential customers, competitors and trends. Define your USP (Unique Selling Point) and when and how you are planning to achieve your targets. A good analysis of the market and strategies that you have put in place to promote your products and services must be defined.

Describe the market analysis against the components listed below, and evaluate your strengths and weaknesses against the competition to identify where you stand in the marketplace.

- Details of competitors
- Health and Safety, and service standards
- Market trends
- Overall size of the market
- Potential customers

11) Marketing Plan

Once you have a clear marketing strategy in place, a detailed marketing plan must be generated. This section of the business plan, must essentially describe how you will achieve marketing targets and objectives within given time-scales.

Here, the business owners must be sensible, but modest about the funds that they make available for the whole marketing process.

And they must ensure that the entire marketing budget is not spent too early.

In general, a good marketing plan would include;

a) Marketing methods
b) Time scales
c) Estimated costs
d) How you will monitor and review progress
e) 4 'P's – product, price, promotion and place

> *Tip: It is important to know the strategies involved, and have accurately balanced components and the correct 'marketing mix', for the business to move forward.*

12) Sales Targets and Objectives

Once your marketing plan is implemented, you need to set out your sales forecast, sales targets and sales objectives on this part of the business plan. Once the business is up and running, after an accurate review, you will be able to know if the targets have been met and accomplished. If they have, then you can set further objectives, explore new ideas and change the business plan accordingly.

13) Operational Requirements and Process

In this section, you need to summarise your plans in terms of the following aspects of your business, stating the estimated costs involved for each aspect. It is vital to ensure that all your resources and equipment are up to date and all operational requirements are at a satisfactory level at all times, to be able to run your business effectively.

Manage the following assets systematically and in order, and keep a record of their details.

- Equipment
- Licensing
- Premises
- Staff
- Suppliers

The operational process must explain details of direct manufacturing of the product or initiation of the service. This may include details from basic ordering of raw materials, forming the team, through to all of the production and servicing stages.

14) Financial Requirements and Forecasts

Knowing what your financial requirements are, how you are planning to fund those requirements, and how you are going to raise further finances you may need, is important at the early stages of any business. Carry out an assessment of the financial situation of your business in the following areas, identify which areas are facing the highest risks and find solutions to them soon, before your business runs out of cash.

- The start-up costs, which are generally high
- Personal financial circumstances
- Details of additional finances available
- A plan detailing what you would be spending finances on
- Estimated break-even point
- Monthly financial forecasts

Including a detailed summary of any previous financial statements, cash flow forecasts, profit and loss accounts and balanced sheets will be useful here too.

Setting out details of existing finances available such as banks, overdrafts, bank loan/s and increased overdrafts in this section, along with time periods, sources of repayment and profit and loss forecasts will be helpful, in case the business needs to raise further funds.

> *Tip : If you are seeking finance then you should not be afraid to offer a share in your business to the investor. Owning part of a successful business is better than owning 100% of a business that has insufficient capital.*

15) Business Risks and Evaluation

Generally your business plan should include an assessment of risks involved within your business and information on how to minimise them.

Take into consideration which of the following risks is more applicable to your business. Implementing strategies to reduce the damaging impact of these risks on the business is beneficial to any entrepreneur.

a) Lack of management experience
b) Little trading history
c) Over reliance on staff and suppliers
d) Over reliance on small customer base
e) Customer debts
f) Increased competition
g) Security issues
h) Political instability
i) Economic uncertainties

It is also important to state details of what might happen in the event of variations in the business plan forecasts, and what could be done to minimise the risks to the business and the investor.

16) SWOT Analysis

Here, you must involve the use of a Strengths, Weaknesses, Opportunities and Threats analysis in your business plan, in order for the business to run more effectively.

- **Strengths** – Your advantages and what you do well.

- **Weaknesses –** What you do badly, what could be improved, and what should be avoided.

- **Opportunities –** The trends in the market, the options you might have and how the market can be exploited to bring something new to it.

- **Threats –** Your competition, the difficulties you are facing and how new entrants have affected your market.

S — what are your advantages? what is it that you do well?

W — what could be improved? what is it that you do badly? what should be avoided?

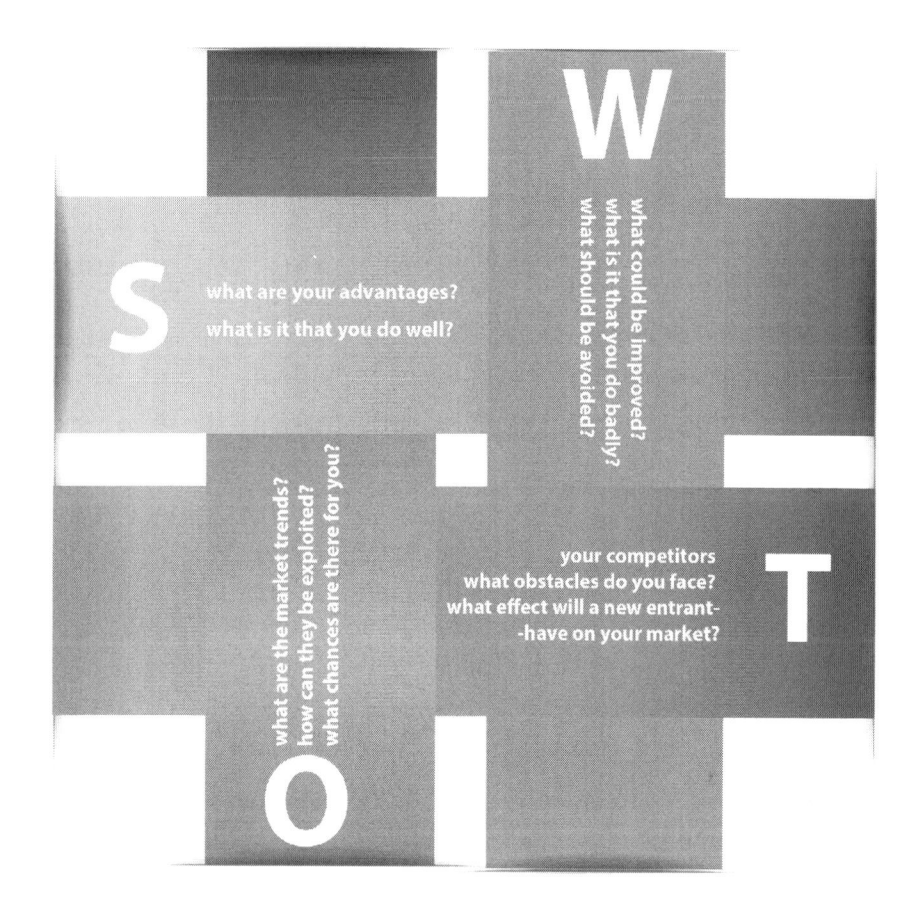

O — what are the market trends? how can they be exploited? what chances are there for you?

T — your competitors, what obstacles do you face? what effect will a new entrant have on your market?

SWOT Analysis

Additionally, the marketing strategy you are planning to employ in your business must look at these 5 key components, and they should describe:

a) **Customers** – Who you are going to sell your products and services to.
b) **Product or Service** – The description and comparison to any existing product or service in the market.
c) **Price** – How much will be charged, how this figure has been calculated and how it compares to competition.

d) **Promotion** – How the business will promote its products and services and how much it will cost and over what period.
e) **Place** – Where the business is based and how the products or services will be distributed or offered.

It is a well-known fact that every business should be aware of Strengths, Weaknesses, Opportunities and Threats associated with it. Knowing them early will help keep the business from prematurely failing. And knowing them early will also help you progress faster and avoiding any potential pitfalls. Furthermore, this analysis will bring to your attention the issues you may face at a very early stage, and offer you a chance to build and improve upon the business strategies you have in place.

> *Tip: SWOT analysis aims to build on strengths, resolve weaknesses, exploit opportunities and avoid threats.*

Appendices in Your Business Plan

Finally, it is essential to include a section for appendices in your business plan. This should include all the documents that support your business plan such as:

a) Your CV
b) CVs of your team
c) Certificates of training courses
d) Copies of leasing, rental agreement of business premises
e) Market research data
f) Financial information

> *Tip 1: Get a friend or relative to read your business plan to you. Ask for their honest feedback. Take their opinion into account. Consider changing your plan if necessary. It is absolutely essential to change the plan and simplify the content, if what is written is not understood by anyone who is reading it.*

> *Tip 2: The presentation of your business plan is essential to make a good first impression, especially when you are meeting with your potential investors. Type your business plan clearly using an attractive and easy to read font and use bold headings. Have a front cover with your contact details clearly shown. Keep in mind that illustrations and short sentences will make the contents much easier to read.*

In summary, a good business plan will:

- Be the most important SALES document you could produce.
- Provide a framework for the business over the coming years in order for the business to develop.
- Be used as a basis for discussion with third parties who have a potential interest in the business.
- Set goals and objectives against which actual performance can be measured and re-evaluated.
- Help you to clarify, focus and research further development of the business.

Therefore, a business plan is essential for any new business to help turn its ideas into a reality.

∞

Common Mistakes to Avoid in a Business Plan

Around 80% of businesses fail, often due to lack of preparation. A business plan will create awareness as to where the business is going, whether sufficient finances are available and how the funds will be invested. In addition, a good plan identifies strengths and weaknesses of the business early, and recommends solutions to limitations, while improving upon strengths. It is common for a new business owner to misjudge or misunderstand statistics, figures and business-related information, as a result of a lack of previous business experience and knowledge. An incorrect and misinterpreted plan will be of no use to you or your business.

Therefore, make sure you avoid these common mistakes at all costs, when drafting the business plan for your new business venture.

1) Unrealistic Financial Projections

A key area of focus in a business plan is the numbers. Knowing your numbers to a greater degree will help you recognise the projected income, estimated profits or losses at the beginning. These numbers need to be credible and consistent. New owners often make the incorrect assumption that a start-up will make profits fast.

It is anticipated that entrepreneurs will over estimate the costs and gains in the first few years of business. A good business plan must include reasonable cost evaluations, correctly estimated break-even points, a return on investment and financial projections to display accurate future financials, and also to identify potential future financial risks.

2) Lack of Clarity

Many business plan recipients such as investors and banks will mostly study the Executive Summary and Financials and decide whether to read further or not. Therefore, a business plan needs to clearly detail business opportunities and display the company's capacity to deliver what is required of it, while catering to the right market, at the right time and at the right cost and this needs to be clearly shown in the Executive Summary and financials.

3) No Clear Understanding of the Market

A well-defined business plan must display how the business intends to reach its customer base. A realistic analysis of how the company plans to access their target market is always important for business growth and to move forward.

Being loyal to your potential customers and being dedicated to them, will lay the foundation for a strong long-term relationship and regular interaction with your consumers will help you to build trust.

4) Poor Cash Flow Management

Many new businesses fail because they are unable to pay their debts. A well-structured business plan needs to explain realistic cash flow projections and potential losses in the initial stages of trading. Realistic financial plans such as planned overdrafts, loans and investment funds should be put in place, well in advance. Managing your cash flow efficiently is vital for business survival.

Getting the cash flow right in the first place, and constantly improving on cash flow strategies is important, while properly restructuring debts through careful planning, to typically reduce bad debt fast.

5) Unsatisfactory Demand

Unless there is demand for your products and services nobody will want to invest in your business, especially if the initial start-up costs are sky high. First, test your business idea on the actual market place while comparing similar businesses in the area. Be conscious about the customer buying behaviours, patterns and trends. Clearly and correctly identify the customers' demands before embarking on your business journey.

6) Playing Down the Competition

There is always competition for any type of business in any part of the world. Identify your competitors early on. Then, you need to recognise what differentiates you from the competition, and evaluate your USP accordingly. Never underestimate the power of your immediate competition. Gear up to face your competition, and prepare for the battle by improving on your strong points and assets.

Therefore, as a new business owner, you must make sure that you avoid these common mistakes at all costs, for long-term survival.

------------ ≈≈≈≈ ------------

« CHAPTER – 3 »

Starting–Up

Starting a new company is difficult, but very exciting. This challenging path an entrepreneur takes can be full of risks and dangers. However, being your own boss can be very rewarding and self-employment is an appealing life style.

When starting off on your mission towards a promising business journey, you must distinguish between your business and personal aims. Establishing realistic business and personal goals at the end of every month or business term is helpful for any member of your team.

The business that needs the most careful planning is the one you start from scratch. No matter how confident you are about your market research, you are never going to be sure how good the idea is, until you are actually up and running. At this stage, good decision making skills and a great deal of patience are vital to keep going.

Discovering the latest business concepts, gathering information and learning about the latest interactive tools available in the market are invaluable for new business owners.

If you are offering a new service or a product with a difference, you will probably grow slowly at first, while your market learns about you. But, this slow growth may be steady, which is vital for long-term survival. An entirely new business with an entirely new approach may be the best way to go. A service or product that already exists may have lot of competition. However, if you can offer products and services with better quality at a reasonable price tag this could be the competitive advantage for your business which could make the difference.

When times are tough and the economy is slowing down, careful planning and clear thinking are fundamental decisive factors for survival.

However, bear in mind those times of great difficulty are also times of great opportunity.

∞

Getting Your Business Off the Ground

Starting a business is hard and challenging. Everyone knows that setting up a business is tough, even before they begin. When it comes to initiating a new business, there isn't just one way to get it off the ground.

But, there are several areas that one must look at, and many people to talk to, just to discover if the business you are planning to launch is feasible or not.

Therefore, before starting out, you must take the following fundamental steps to strengthen your business's focus and to ensure that it is protected from any potential losses.

• Self - Employment – The Secret to Success •

Keeping Your Business on Track

1) Take Advice

Always seek expert advice and support, in all aspects of your business. Getting the right guidance, especially as you are starting out, is very important. Therefore, involve your family, get information from government authorities in your area, plug into business networks, participate in business conversation in forums or take appropriate advice from anyone who is already running a business; all of these will be useful.

Also, look for opportunities at local business networks in your area or on the web, find as many network groups as possible and get advice, share knowledge and experiences. Obtaining such information will be invaluable at any stage of the business.

2) Identify the Best Finance Options

Calculate how much funding you will need to start and run your business, at least for the first year. Ideally you want to secure funding for up to five years. You may be able to borrow from friends and family, use savings, use government-backed support schemes or seek financial assistance from investors. Work out the best, most affordable and safest option for you. In the meantime, speaking to your local bank manager and seeking help to increase the overdraft facility, increasing the limit on your credit card, applying for a new credit card or a bank loan can be useful, too. However, it is also essential to estimate when you would be able to repay the debts, well before running into much larger and unaffordable financial situations.

Get regular advice from your accountant and local council on how to obtain financial help or how to obtain crowd funding facilities available to small local businesses. Also you must not forget to negotiate with your suppliers or the middle man to get better quotes, to cut down on costs involved.

Never forget that, you must always **'Ask to Receive!'**

Ascertaining the general costs involved, on a daily, weekly or monthly basis to run your business, and knowing the break-even points extremely well is important.

3) Formulate Sales and Marketing Strategies

When you have a service or product to sell, you must prepare and implement an effective marketing plan to take it forward. Also identifying the most suitable, efficient and effective sales mediums to reach your target market is crucial for a new entrepreneur. A great marketing plan will result in improved profitability, productivity and overall business success. Therefore, making sure you build up an impressive profile for the business and recognising who your customers are, where they are, and what they want, will help you stay ahead of your direct competition.

Good sales and marketing strategies are essential to take your business to higher levels. Marketing prepares your products and services to meet your customers' needs. Designing exciting materials and utilising reliable marketing mediums to promote your business will cost money, but you must never forget that the benefits they can offer you will certainly outweigh these costs.

Great marketing plans raise the value of your products or services and encourage potential customers to buy from you. Also, you need to ensure that your sales systems and channels are well placed, and that they are user friendly, enabling people to buy your products or services easily without a hassle.

If your initial marketing strategies are not working, you should immediately take steps to stop or change them to suit the current needs of the market and its trends.

Do not stick to one plan. Keep exploring!

However, you must not underestimate the important role your personal contacts and word-of-mouth referrals can play; they could effectively improve your presence in today's competitive market-place.

4) Analyse Your Personality and Recruit the Right Staff

As discussed earlier, you need to ask yourself if you have the personality, the desire, the drive and enthusiasm not only to start a business, but also to make it a success. Creating a checklist of your personal attributes including what you can and cannot do, will help you identify the best qualities you can capitalise on for the progress of your business. Also, write down the objectives of starting the business, stick up motivational pictures or quotes in the work place and set up inspirational screensavers on your computers or mobile to keep you and your team inspired throughout the day, and to bring out the best, in everyone.

Furthermore, you must identify the areas of the business where you will need expert skills. Employ people with the right attitude and relevant experience if you can afford to do so, or involve family and friends who can support you, to improve those areas. Making sure your team shares the same vision as you, is imperative, to direct them towards the same goal and mission. Listen to what your team has to say, involve them in decision making, and also share the rewards with them.

5) Involve Family and Earn Their Support

Explain to your family members the importance and difficulties of running a business. Share your dream with them. Take regular advice from them. See the bigger picture together. Appreciate their input towards the progress of the business. Spend time with your family to strengthen the relationship, as they will be the most affected by every good or bad action you take in relation to your business.

On the other hand, your family could offer moral support when you are under immense pressure or keep an eye on the finances for you. They will be sharing your future worries and accomplishments for the most part. So remember, they are the most important people in your life, Right Now!

Therefore, your home atmosphere should be very supportive, especially in the early and most difficult stages of your business.

Consider yourself lucky if you have your family's full approval and support for your decision to become self-employed. It is your responsibility to let them know about the consequences that they might have to face, when you are working long hours and having stressful, sleepless nights. Your family needs to understand the risks and lower income that your business may bring, at the beginning.

So, have frequent conversations with your family to share your problems or achievements and get their advice and thoughts for improvement. You may even find out things you would not have noticed if it wasn't for your family. They might look at things with a different perspective to yours. However, in case if they all offer conflicting advice, or don't have a business head, seeking independent expert and objective advice may be helpful.

Keep in mind that, every little bit of advice counts!

> *Tip: Carry out a critical assessment of your abilities and skills. Talk to your family or hire an expert and get their support on areas where necessary.*

6) Customer Service Plan

The customer is the key player of your business's growth and sustainability. So your business must be planned while keeping your customers in mind. Do your research on consumer markets, their requirements and methods to impress, and make your mark on the world of business. Your products and services should be aimed at providing the best possible customer care.

Make your customers come back for more. Failing to appreciate the value of an exceptional customer service plan, will strongly affect your future sales, due to declining visits and negative word of mouth.

When adding new products or services to your business, you must never disregard customer views, the experiences of your sales team or neglect the opinion of focus groups.

Gathering as much information as possible from every source available to you, will help you understand the market you are in, and also make you more aware of your competition.

Offering the best product or service to your customers at affordable costs, and on time, is invaluable. Also, making arrangements for prompt refunds, disclosing certain procedures and policies you may have to take, and being open and honest about it with your customers, are all priceless customer service strategies that you might need to consider putting into practice.

7) Find the Right Location

Choosing the right location means, taking into account a number of factors. This decision must be carefully considered, taking into account details such as, premises costs, competitors, running costs and accessibility for potential clients. Also, it is important to consider the type of image you wish to promote through your business premises and type of people you employ. Additionally, the location where your customers are based is important too. Your priority must be to go to your customer, not wait for your customer to come to you.

Some small businesses can be operated from home, which greatly reduces the initial overhead costs. If you are unable to see your customers from the comfort of your home, then you can book a hotel, business club or temporary meeting area as a short-term solution. These days, there are number of small office spaces available for booking, in prominent areas in many cities on a short-term contract.

Make use of all the opportunities available to you.

Most importantly, make sure the place you have chosen, is the right location for your business.

The classic advice "location, location, location" is right on the mark, as it can make a real difference to the success of your business.

8) Use Technology

Most businesses could not operate without appropriate use of technology in today's fast-moving commercial world. Nowadays all-in-one, network ready multifunctional quality printers, scanners, copiers and fax machines with wi-fi are seamlessly integrated into current business systems and ideal for any office environment. Also, don't forget the widespread use of smartphone and tablets within a business and by its customers. And certainly the latest computers will also help maintain communication at a satisfactory level to explore opportunities, improve efficiency and keep your books up to date.

Right now, email is commonly used and considered as the most popular communication tool by business owners, suppliers and customers at all levels. Customers in the modern world prefer video chat or online chat before making a purchase on the Internet, because it saves them time, travel and hassle.

Utilising the latest technology can result in improved accuracy, efficiency and effective communication, which are important for your business's growth. Good use of technology can positively influence the way your business is operated. Therefore, it is time for you to embrace innovative technology and incorporate the latest 'gadgets' when and where you possibly can. Think of technology as an essential marketing tool for your business.

9) Bookkeeping

Bookkeeping is a crucial element of any business. Many small business owners end up managing the accounts themselves, especially when first starting out. However, it is believed that using the services of an accountant you can trust and rely on, or using the assistance of someone who can genuinely advise you on the financial aspects to help you manage your accounts accurately, is more effective than managing the accounts yourself. Accurate accounting is a vital part of running a business effectively. Most businesses fail when the owners lose track of their numbers and do not realise they are running at a loss until it is too late.

Initially, you may be able to record your purchases, sales and all transactions on MS Excel, before moving into more complicated versions of software packages that are available. Keeping all your transactions recorded very clearly on a simple platform will help you identify your financial situation and the cash position of your business precisely and accurately at any stage of the business.

Ideally you should obtain the services of an accountant to do the yearly accounts and to collaborate with the tax office on your behalf. This will leave you with more time to focus on what you are good at. Generally, a professional will be able to discover how profitable or unprofitable your business really is, much quicker than you do.

However, with or without your accountant's help, you must know your books and numbers well enough to be able to progress on to the next level.

10) Know the Law and Your Taxes

Make sure you correctly understand the law and legal requirements of starting and running a business. This includes knowing about your taxes, VAT registration and relevant insurance policies. The legal requirements differ from one company to another depending on the legal status of the business such as, sole trader, limited company, partnership, clubs, societies or associations. Also, take into account health and safety and employment law in relation to your business. Consult your accountant or solicitor for good tips on business law and finance that are relevant to you.

It is also worth noting that rules and regulations could differ from country to country, region to region, or location to location. Be aware of the law that might be affecting your business at both local and global level.

It is also useful to know consumer law and regulations, when you are using social media and the Internet for your business needs. Furthermore, contact your tax office and register your business as soon as things are up and running.

By failing to do so, you might face very large fines. By law, as a self-employed person you must complete tax returns every year.

It is useful to keep track of the dates that you are planning to see your accountant to discuss tax payment plans for the financial year. You should be able to organise relevant invoices, receipts and all related documentation and keep them in order, in preparation for the year-end accounts.

Planning your finances early will avoid unnecessary errors, and it will also help you to escape the last-minute rush of filing your tax return. As discussed above, take advice from an accountant who will be able to assist you with your accounts and deal with your tax affairs.

11) Get Insurance Cover

Self-employment is clearly a challenge and there are unforeseen risks such as flood, fire and theft attached to it, as to any type and size of business. Therefore, it is important to safeguard your business from such disastrous events by taking out an insurance scheme to provide protection.

Make sure your business is covered for the worst case scenario.

Also, there are various different insurance schemes available in the market for employer's liability, public liability, property damage, professional indemnity, income protection, critical illness, etc. You can always consult your local bank, get advice from your accountant or insurance brokers to decide what is right for your business.

Take time to explore all the options suitable for you, your employees and your business in general.

Preparing for Business

The key to success is being able to offer the right product and service to the right market, at the right time. Being aware of your customer needs and competitors, and having a good knowledge of current and historical information about them, will help you forecast accurately, and also recognise future demand. By looking into the following factors, and conducting in-depth research on them, you could prevent your business from an early exit.

a) Your customer base
b) Your product/service and pricing
c) Suitable and affordable location
d) Marketing and advertising strategies
e) Who and where your competition is

The next key to success is to understand your financial capacity. This includes how your finances are met and how long your business can afford to survive on its current financial options. Watching your current economic situation and managing your finances efficiently on a daily/weekly basis will be beneficial. Being acquainted with financial information such as the following will be extremely helpful to any business owner:

- How much start-up capital is invested
- Estimated day-to-day operational costs and income
- When you will reach break-even point
- The likely sales volume for the next few weeks
- The profit level required for the business to survive
- When you are planning to earn satisfactory profit levels

After careful planning, assessing your abilities and finances, carrying out feasibility checks, and reaching out to the market to establish the demand, you should now be ready to get your business off the ground. However, you must always have a watchful eye on every business task and some guidelines in place and strategies involved, to keep yourself on track.

> *Tip: You could always hunt for ideas and opportunities by reading business magazines, newspapers, periodicals, web sites and by visiting exhibitions and seminars especially organised for entrepreneurs etc.*

When your business is up and running, you must constantly be aware of what is happening around you and create to-do lists, note the things you have missed and jot down important information for further improvement. Never be afraid to change the existing strategies and how you do your business entirely, if necessary.

∞

Seven Reasons Why New Businesses Fail

Starting a business from scratch is not an easy mission. According to research, more than 50% of small and new businesses fail in the first couple of years and almost 95% fail within the first five years of trading.

Here are some of the common pitfalls to avoid, as you begin your small business journey.

1) Poor Business Plan

A good business plan covers aspects such as marketing, finance, sales, as well as detailed breakdown of costs and profit predictions. A poor business plan will not pinpoint any of such information accurately, which will be one of the reasons for the business to collapse prematurely. A poorly drafted plan will not help you recognise potential dangers early enough, enabling you to recover from failure.

Many business owners think that their commitment, hard work and passion will take them all the way to success. The truth is that this is not enough. But some good and early planning is certainly essential.

A great plan means that you have carefully looked at all the phases of your business and potential problems are identified well before they arise. Your business plan helps you concentrate on the objectives and vision of your business, while setting out strategies to accomplish them.

2) No Clear Purpose

Lack of clear objectives will waste your time and resources. You must set a clear vision and realistic goals for the business. The changing nature of business means that it is essential for you to maintain regular communication channels with your staff and suppliers to keep them well informed and up to date at all times, to make sure that you always share a common purpose with your team.

Therefore, organisations must have clearly planned out and connected objectives that enable everyone involved in the business, to move forwards in the same direction. That is, the PATH that leads to success!

3) Inadequate Finance and Cash Flow Problems

Insufficient cash flow often means that a business is unable to take the great opportunities available to it. Because of this, businesses tend to stay in one place for a long time, without any measurable progress.

It is a fact that many new businesses struggle as a result of poor finances. Therefore you must be prepared to survive at least a year without any return on your investment. Also, you have to create a realistic financial statement, and keep an eye out for spending on anything beyond basic, essential needs.

At the early stages of the business, it is healthier to control excessive spending in your personal life as well. If you are unable to pay your bills now, you are unable to open your business next month.

Tight control and monitoring is important, to avoid facing potential financial crisis.

4) Weak Management

Weak management is another main reason for early business failure. A good leader must be able to guide his/her team by example and motivate them by recognising talent and rewarding them when necessary. Also, a great manager must be accountable for good or bad decisions taken by him/her in any business situation. The longer your team sticks with you, the healthier the business becomes. Therefore, a good leader must have the skill to improve staff retention to be able to achieve great results.

Successful business owners are great leaders. They inspire their employees, and often acknowledge their good work. By taking steps to improve personal development and team spirit within your team you will help your business to go that extra mile. Remember, your team is one of the greatest assets in your business, as they represent the brand of your business and promote the business's image.

5) Poor Marketing Strategies

Successful businesses take pride in recognising opportunities early and meeting the requirements of their customers. Hence, learning the basics of marketing and implementing a system that can lead to success is essential. You must build marketing strategies that attract your customers and you must clearly define why they would rather come to you than go to a competitor.

If your marketing strategies and techniques are not bringing any sales into the business, you must change them immediately. Recognise the latest trends in the market and adjust your strategies to suit changing needs.

Initially, self-employment is a one-man band. Only a limited time will be available to you to perform several tasks, all by yourself and then with your small team. Certain tasks such as marketing and advertising may require lot of thinking and planning to reach the targeted audience. Failure to diversify marketing channels and marketing material, lack of marketing momentum and of an overall marketing plan will have a bad effect on sales.

6) Failure to Employ New Technologies

Technology has advanced over the years and leading businesses are making the best possible use of new technologies in the most efficient and effective way. That could be one of the reasons why they are at the top of the leader board. If your competitors are using new technology and have found success, then you cannot afford not to use it too.

Currently mobile technology is a booming sector. And it is the right move to make your website, applications and software all mobile compatible. New ideas and innovative technology, will contribute towards your business's competitive edge, enabling you to grow with the market.

Moreover, there is software available for almost every type of business, providing assistance to organise daily tasks, do the accounts, improve efficiency, conduct market research, organise emails, etc. Taking advantage of those software packages that are most suitable to you will make your life simpler, more efficient and a whole lot easier.

7) Wrong Location

As discussed earlier, a good location is imperative to reach large numbers of customers. Therefore you need to make sure that you are well located in relation to your customers and your suppliers or distributors. However, if you are an online business, it might not matter where you are.

It's a good idea to do your sums and work out what you can truly afford before running into large debts by choosing the right location at the wrong cost. Once you have chosen the location that suits you, keep your customers well informed before they make a visit.

Many customers prefer convenience and less hassle over price. If you are based in the wrong location right now, and cannot afford to move to the best location that you would prefer, be patient and you will be there sooner than you think.

Structuring Your Business

The structure of your business needs to be a solid foundation. The structure you choose for your business will depend on the aims, size and nature of the business.

A well-defined organisation structure promotes success. And it is certainly important for the business owners to make sure every single person involved in the business understands their role within the company.

Entrepreneurs are a diverse group and they share a collection of characteristics. And the best ones are:

Common Attributes of a Successful Entrepreneur

It is also a real benefit for entrepreneurs to demonstrate and improve on their personal attributes to be able to progress to the next level of their business. So, make sure you and your team are equipped with these attributes and more, to achieve great success.

As a new business owner, you may not be the perfect candidate to start a business. However, there are many things that you may learn and develop over time. Further to above attributes, these are also considered to be important as you start out your own.

1) Ability to work under severe pressure
2) Fast learning skills
3) Good decision-making skills
4) Motivation and passion

Building up these skills along the way and 'learning as you go' are very commonly practiced in the business world today.

Prompt planning will save your business from potential collapse and early closures. To maximise your chances of success, a number of significant decisions must be made, one of which is choosing great leaders.

Great leadership and a positive attitude go together, and are essential components to build a solid foundation and a strong structure for any business. Good entrepreneurs must always be good leaders and motivators, and they must be able to place people where they will achieve long-term success.

Furthermore, time is valuable when you are concentrating on growing your business. Therefore, it is vital that you are in possession of a clear structure and some measurable, achievable, time-scaled objectives, a system for accurate bookkeeping and a good customer service plan, to stay ahead of the others.

As your business develops your needs will begin to change too.

So, when it is the right time, you must take a moment to understand your business, work with your team and work with relevant specialists to re-evaluate changing business needs, and deal with complex queries there and then.

∞

Pitfalls to Avoid

As a business owner you must always be aware of where your business is currently at, and what your immediate goals are. You must always stop, think and evaluate. Stop, think and evaluate again.

It is always advisable to make every attempt to avoid potential pitfalls, by maintaining a well thought-out operational plan, and accurate business decisions.

Do your research before trying something new and unfamiliar to you. Incorrect decisions you take in stressful situations might not be reversible, may damage your business prospects, and could even result in an unexpected early exit.

Therefore, assessing your abilities well in advance is of paramount importance for business success. And you must carefully look at the following list of problems that cause many small businesses to fail in their initial years.

1) Being overly optimistic about the market
2) Having no clear competitive advantage
3) High initial cost
4) Knowing too little about the market
5) Low start-up budget
6) Low working capital
7) Poor accounting and record keeping
8) Underestimating start-up time
9) Wrong location
10) Wrong people in the team

Ideally, conducting appropriate research and measuring up your capabilities, such as skills, resources and finances will enable you to decide if you are on the right path, and if not, what changes could be made to realise your vision.

« CHAPTER – 4 »

Running Your Business

Success will only come through hard work and offering something that the consumer wants. Wanting to run your own business because you have no other option is definitely not the right reason to become self-employed. It is important to see your own business as an opportunity to do something you really want to do.

What Sort of Business

If you are going to offer something that can be bought elsewhere, then you need to persuade your customers that they should buy from you rather than your competitor. For that, you need to be different from your competition and offer something special to win over the consumers and immediately impress them. The following qualities could make you stand out from the rest in the market:

    a) Better quality
    b) Faster speed of response
    c) Integrity

d) Longer opening hours
e) Lower price

Therefore, instil these qualities into your business to score higher than your competitors in the market.

See, Listen and Learn

As an inexperienced entrepreneur, you tend to make mistakes at the early stages of your business. It is hard to avoid these mistakes at first. But embracing these mistakes that come your way, and being ready to learn from them is what counts.

It is good idea to watch what other people or businesses do, stop and think about why the others are doing what they are doing differently, and adopt those changes, as required if appropriate to your business.

If you ever feel you are not doing the right thing and feel insecure, then it would be beneficial to get a business mentor involved. A mentor is an outsider. He or she may be able to see what you cannot see and identify certain areas of concern.

A mentor is an experienced person who can simply transfer his/her knowledge to running your business. He or she could even keep you motivated on your challenging journey.

Also it is fundamental to speak to your partner, parents and trusted friends and get their opinions, ideas and suggestions for improvement at any stage of your business. However, you should be able to choose only the advice appropriate to your business as they may all give you conflicting or bad advice.

Working From Home

Running your business from home at the beginning of your journey will save you a great deal of money and time. It is a known fact that working from home contributes towards maintaining a good work-life balance and saving considerable overhead costs.

Working from Home

Working from home today, has become very efficient and productive and more feasible, given the advances in technology. The latest technology and the Internet have made 'effective' working from home a reality.

These modern 'smarter' working practices promote flexibility while enabling you to cut down on costs. However, as the business expands, you may need to consider moving into a suitable office space to achieve greater exposure.

Purchasing Items

As a new business, you will need to purchase items, materials, furniture, etc for the business to function. Do your research and decide what items are best suited to the business, and spend wisely.

Allocate a reasonable budget and stick to it without spending over the limit on unnecessary office items. Generally, buying items over the Internet is cheaper than buying from high street shops. Your local auction house is another place where you could fetch a bargain and freecycle in the UK where you could even get free office furniture that someone is getting rid of. Streetbank is another movement of people in the UK who share things and offer items for free or to lend, or offer skills. Therefore, it is a good idea to look for similar places in your country/area to buy things where there are plenty of useful and inexpensive items.

Furthermore, be aware of the guarantee/warranty period of the products and their refundable policies. Also take in to account the delivery charges and how many days it will take to deliver items to your doorstep.

All these are significant initial concerns that would matter, when setting up a work space.

Train Your Team

It is vital for a growing company to conduct training sessions to constantly improve the quality of its work. Regular information sharing and team building exercises will improve morale and also keep your employees up to date.

This will greatly influence your employees' self-confidence and team spirit. And in turn, these higher engagement levels will result in higher productivity.

Successful business owners are great leaders. It is the duty of great leaders to find time, attend to any special requests of the team, listen to what they have to say and do the best they can to keep them in the business as long as they can.

Training your team as required will enable your employees to perform the tasks assigned to them to the best of their ability. Make your team feel that they are a valuable asset to you and your business.

Your team is a vital part of your business. So it is important to treat them appropriately to ensure long-term growth.

∞

Setting Objectives

As a business owner you must ensure that the objectives you have set for your enterprise are SMART. It is time to assess for yourself if these objectives, targets and goals are specific, measurable, achievable, realistic and timed.

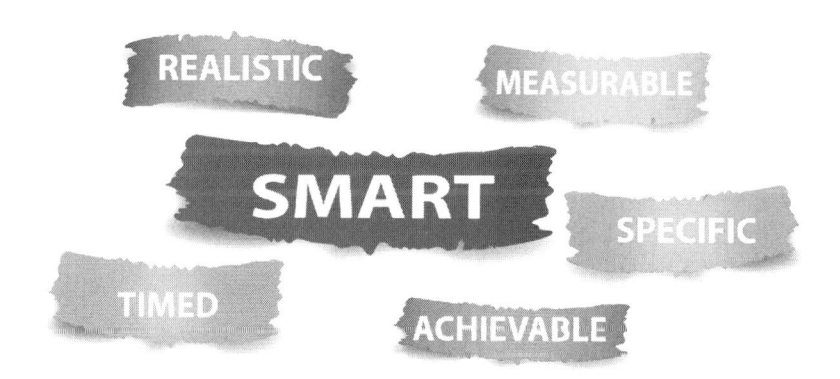

SMART Objectives

> **Tip:** *In your first year of trading your only objective may be to make sufficient profit to enable you to achieve an acceptable standard of living. However, the years following this should be 'SMART'er.*

- Specific   –   S
- Measurable   –   M
- Achievable   –   A
- Realistic   –   R
- Timed   –   T

Precise and prompt monitoring and control of all business functions will inevitably ensure greater outcome within the overall business. By keeping an eye on the following you will be able to identify the areas that need further development.

a) Changes in efficiency
b) Changes in productivity
c) Changes in profitability
d) Advanced technology requirements

By focusing your business objectives on your customers, all else is sure to follow. Therefore, it is necessary for budding entrepreneurs to understand what their business is all about, have clear objectives and identify where they want to be in five years.

Generally, as your business begins to grow, the number of objectives and goals increases as well. As a result of this, certain business functions must also transform accordingly. Keeping an eye on every part of your business operation and conducting necessary reviews on them is essential.

Your Business Strategy

In addition to setting up objectives, an efficient use of PESTE analysis would also provide a focused framework for general business activities.

- Political   –   P
- Economic   –   E
- Social   –   S
- Technological   –   T
- Environmental   –   E

It is worthwhile evaluating the current political, economic, social and environmental situation around your business, in addition to carrying out an appropriate technological assessment.

It is very important for the business owner to correctly understand their market position during the early stages.

And it is important not to underestimate the significant value of the above components and know their role in your business, to trade effectively.

Threats

Threats are potential risks to your business and necessary precautions to prevent them from happening must be taken from very early on. Some of those threats that may harm your overall business would be:

a) **Substitute products or services** – Alternative products and services might be easily available for the consumer. Therefore, you must find your USP to fight back.

b) **Government/tax policies** – Regular changes may occur. Be attentive to changing regulations and investigate what your current legal and business requirements are, and abide by their policies, so that you aren't negatively affected.

c) **Power of suppliers and buyers** – The less suppliers and customers you have, the more power they are likely to have over your business. Therefore, by increasing your supplier and customer numbers, you would not need to depend on one supplier for too long and you could negotiate a better deal with a range of suppliers. Also, by increasing your customer base, your business would be less vulnerable if your biggest customer left you.

d) **New entrants** – New competition. You will need to have clear strategies to avoid damaging impact to the business.

e) **Extent of competitive rivalry** – Differentiate your business from your competitors and find your competitive advantage to avoid being marginalised.

∞

Market Research

Extensive market research is vital for a start-up to find out what customers want to buy, why they buy the products/services they buy, when they buy and where they buy from. Then segment your customers based on age, occupation, standard of education, income levels, and marital status and, most importantly, the location.

From intensive market research, you may be able to collect and analyse data and information that is valuable to your business, and examine it to determine certain trends and patterns in the market. Such information would be an extremely valuable asset for any growing company.

Conducting your own market research has never been easier. Online tools mean that anyone can conduct their own research at their own pace. It is always wise to keep yourself up to date about the changing market atmosphere.

Paying attention to who your competitors are, details of their business, location, their products and services, their customers, the pricing and particularly their changing circumstances will be helpful for any business owner in the long run.

Market research will give you an overview of what consumers' want and what they aspire to. Conducting intensive research will determine how and where a product or service could be best marketed. It is also important to get advice on how to reach more customers from professionals in the field.

Intensive Market Research

Tip: Set yourself tasks to do. Research the market on a regular basis to stay ahead of the competition.

Competition

Your competitors are your rivals. In general, there are four main types of competition and it makes sense to know who they are, to get an accurate picture of the market you are in.

- **Direct** – These are the companies that offer the same products or services as you. And these are your BIGGEST rivals.

- **Indirect** – Companies that operate in different markets, but offer products that can easily be converted or reach into your market.

- **Linked** – Businesses that offer the same service but deliver in a different market.

- **Industry** – These are businesses that offer the same product area but sell in different markets.

So watch out! Any one of the above could become your BIGGEST competition, sooner than you think.

∞

Staying Ahead

As a new business owner, keeping ahead of the competition is not an easy task. To do this, one has to perform one's task well, typically using the market knowledge, by following consumer trends and investing in new technology.

One of the most important responsibilities of a small business owner is to make sure that they live out 'the mantra' for tough economic times, 'the survival of the fittest', to stay ahead of the competition.

Also, business owners need to anticipate change at all times, and adapt to such changes promptly, if they want to succeed.

The following are some of the key actions to pursue if you are hoping to become the next market leader.

1) Discover Your Competitive Advantage

Differentiating the services and products you offer through longer opening hours, improved delivery, and the right price, and by aiming for measurable differences in quality, will give you a good chance to establish your USP in the market that you operate in.

Do whatever you can to offer the best product or service possible to your customers at all times.

Value every idea and suggestion of your customers as their views may help shape what your business already does.

Answer customer queries, phone calls and respond to emails or texts efficiently, to make the customers feel that you are approachable at any given time. Showcase the fact that you are an honest and transparent business. Recommend what you believe to be the best for your customer. Think about all the little things you can do to improve loyalty.

So, make sure you are in possession of these success factors to boost customer satisfaction:

- High quality products and services
- Competitive pricing
- Better speed of delivery

2) Manage Finance Effectively

Find out the most productive ways of delivering your service or product to your customers. Using your time efficiently, allocating your resources effectively, and managing finances accurately from the early days can lead to the achievement of greater outcomes.

> **Tip:** Setting up plans to increase efficiency in all business tasks will lead to lower costs of production and a lower selling price.

3) Market Research

Intensive market research will enable you to update your sales forecasts on a regular basis, keep track of competitors and obtain feedback from your customers. Recognising the changing business environment at any stage of the business is essential for growth.

4) Avoid Complacency

There will always be something that you can do better or more efficiently. Never assume that you have done your bit and achieved your full potential. Look for ways for further development and growth in all areas of business. Seek to improve quality and service all the time, while providing what your customers want, at the right price and right time.

And the satisfied customers will put your name on the map!

Buyer Behaviour

It is essential to understand the 'buying behaviour' of your potential customers to ensure that you are offering what your customers want. It is believed that the customers become more comfortable and confident in their ability to find the best product, at the best price, from a seller that they can trust.

In addition to understanding the needs of your customers, you also need to understand what motivates them to buy and how emotions affect their buying patterns. It is also essential to analyse the purchasing habits of your potential buyers clearly, as the consumers' buying process can be a complex matter.

Current consumers are savvy, and they tend to have more control over what you sell. Also there is so much choice in terms of everything that is available today which has made the competition increase immensely.

Equally, consumers nowadays like to choose convenience over price. Therefore, it has become more difficult for business owners to survive within this volatile marketplace.

As customers continue to have more power of choice, the business world moves into a new era of three Cs: Choice, Convenience and Control. Therefore, anyone who is a new entrant to the market must always be aware of all these important factors before beginning to trade.

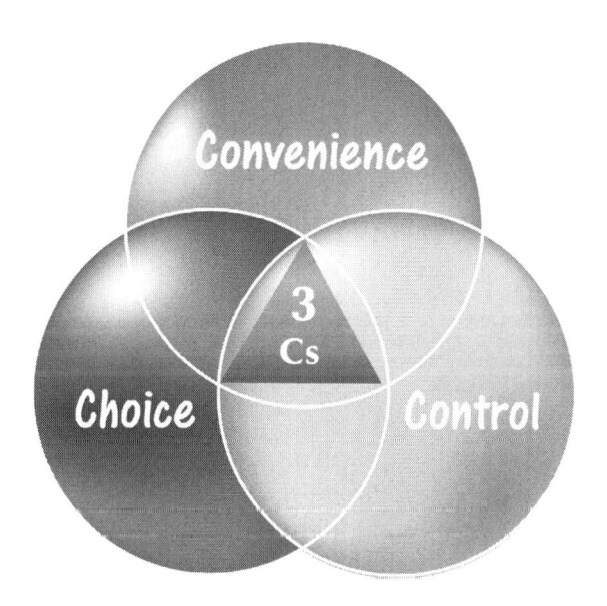

Three Cs

The Pricing

Before setting up prices on your products or services, it is crucial to identify the buying patterns of your customer and how your competitors are pricing their products and services.

It is apparent that 'The Price' of a product or service could make or break a deal. Correctly and reasonably priced items contribute towards that important purchasing decision of the customer.

Therefore, ideally you need to read your consumer's mind and set up pricing correctly, before putting your products and services on sale.

The following describes the general thinking patterns of consumers in relation to pricing, and would be exceptionally useful for anyone starting out:

a) Usually, the consumer does have a vague idea about the true price. Even though it may not be known, it is not ideal to price your products and services excessively high.

b) Changing the prices frequently might cause confusion among consumers, and they may become suspicious and not buy from you.

c) Occasional small price reductions would seem to be an offering of better value. Therefore customers tend to make a purchase.

d) Large discounts make the consumer think that the product could be outdated. These products will be rejected, for the most part.

e) A reduced price can mean that there is something not right with the product/service and consumers are likely to refuse to buy.

f) 'Cut price' discounts may mean that further reductions will follow. Therefore, the purchasing decisions of consumers will be delayed.

Complaints

Always consider a complaint as an opportunity.

Therefore, take customer complaints seriously and handle them as soon as you can. Exceptional complaint handling is not easy, and can often be stressful and feel unrewarding. Handling customer complaints quickly, correctly and professionally is an extremely important aspect of any business organisation.

Gaining a reasonable knowledge of how to handle complaints efficiently is necessary for a company wanting to remain competitive.

It would be valuable to learn about your buyer's behaviour on making a complaint, in order to handle it effectively.

- 25% of consumers are not satisfied but will not make a complaint.
- Only 5% of your customers will actually make a complaint.
- 50% are satisfied with the way complaints are handled.
- Satisfied customers will tell only ONE person about you.
- Dissatisfied customers will tell FOUR people about you.

One of the most critical factors in complaint handling is the ability to demonstrate that you have acknowledged the complaint, and promise the customer to successfully resolve the matter soon. Also, do not forget to get the customer's feedback after the complaint has been resolved.

And finally, never be afraid to apologise.

> *Tip: It is extremely important that you have a strategy in place to deal with complaints, and deal with them professionally and fast.*

Importance of Promotion

The truth is, in this fiercely competitive world, 'being good' simply isn't enough. Instead, you need to be the BEST.

Most marketing and promotional strategies are closely interlinked, and need to be activated to make your business well known in the market you operate in, and to be accepted by your consumers. Therefore, it is essential for new owners to take every potential opportunity to promote their business in every possible manner.

Often, social conversations at events turn to what you do for a living and you may gain a potential customer in this way. This method of promotion can be used at occasions such as a wedding, a birthday party, or any social or personal gathering. Take every opportunity that occurs, to gradually build up your customer numbers.

As an entrepreneur, carrying a supply of business cards, marketing materials and promotional supplies relevant to your business, when you go out socially is a simple way of promoting what you do.

And this is what you must do, when you meet prospective customers, and typically this is what many business owners have done during their initial years of trading:

- Make them aware of your existence.
- Introduce your products and services to them.
- Explain and convince them of how your products and services will satisfy their needs.
- Help them decide that your products and services are the best, to suit their needs.
- Positively persuade them to make a purchase.

Tip: Consider very carefully the message that you want to send to your customers. Because once the message is released, it is too late to make any changes.

The Marketing

You need to frequently remind people that you exist. Promote your products and services by carefully selecting different advertising media on a regular basis.

Choose the communication channels best suited to you to pass on your message. The best practice is to set objectives when you are preparing for the BIG promotion.

These objectives you set, before launching any type of promotional campaign, are all about:

- Introducing a product or service to existing and new customers
- Highlighting features, benefits, quality of a product or service
- Drawing consumer attention to discounts or special offers
- Retaining and building upon the brand image
- Reminding customers about your existence
- Increasing awareness of improved quality of a product or service
- Stimulating repeat business

These days, diverse promotional activities are practised within most successful businesses. They are keen to accelerate their strategies to stay ahead of competition and the methods described below are commonly used to promote what is offered to the potential markets.

1) Personal Selling

This is selling directly to the consumer using personal contacts or word of mouth.

Personal selling can be achieved by face-to-face meetings, over the telephone, at trade fairs and exhibitions or by email, if you are already known to the consumer in some way.

Consider these as priceless opportunities to make a good sale.

2) Sales Promotions

These promotional activities include offering discount vouchers, free samples of your product or a free initial consultation of your services. This type of sales promotions will create repeat customers, provided that you offered an excellent first service or product and the customers were satisfied with it. It is very important to know how to build a customer base that will keep coming back to you, and stick with you for a long time.

3) Advertising

Advertising in the right medium, to ensure that your advert will not be out of place, is invaluable. Choose the right advertising channel for your target market, ascertain its value for the money you pay and make sure the advertising medium you have chosen is seen by targeted customers. High cost TV or radio adverts might not be suitable for you at the early stages of the business.

Consequently, it is a good idea to explore free advertising media in your area. Make sure you do not spend hugely on just advertising before you make any money.

Watch your finances frequently, as it is easy to run out of money without realising it when it comes to advertising.

4) PR Activities and Publicity

The most ideal first approach for PR is to contact the business editor of your local newspaper if you have something interesting, exciting and newsworthy for the public. Depending on how remarkable the news or advert is, the editor might somehow find space for you in the immediate publication. If they don't have space for your item now, they may feature your business idea, advert, or news in a future release.

And you must not take too lightly the power of such free editorial coverage, and the awareness it can bring into your business. It can certainly do more for your business than a paid advertisement.

When you are introducing your new business to the market it is greatly recommended that you invite your local councillor or mayor, well-known individuals in the community, journalists, and photographers, to get additional and very significant free publicity.

The initial steps you choose to take are crucial for a fresh business to succeed or fail. Your sales promotions must be targeted to attract new customers rather than to allure existing customers to eventually build up your overall customer base.

> *Tip: Whatever promotional techniques you have chosen, make sure that you give your customers time to think. Advertising doesn't always work overnight. Make sure you deliver exactly what you say you will deliver on your adverts.*

∞

Using Technology in Your Business

Reducing delay, sourcing to optimise and improving communication are critical to any business's survival. Using innovative technology in the business will help you do just that. There are resource planning tools and management software available in the market today, which can bring in cost savings by monitoring performance of almost all business tasks effectively. By utilising these latest tools and technologies in your business, more competitive products and services can be offered, thereby capturing a greater market share and customer loyalty.

Whatever kind of business you are running, it is ideal to have a full computer system implemented to achieve greater productivity. Various types of easy-to-use software packages, tools and applications can be carefully selected to help you carry out day-to-day operation more effectively.

There are applications for bookkeeping, business planning, data back-up, legal compliance, e-learning and website building to choose from.

Making use of business software packages and advanced technology in any part of your business will offer benefits such as:

- Ability to organise all correspondence, marketing materials and customer databases into one place
- Ability to keep duplicate records and have at least three back-up copies stored in different places for safety
- Cost savings on accountancy charges
- Less time spent 'doing the books' and faster production of accounts
- Benefits such as automatic creation of letterheads and invoices in a standardised format
- Training software for staff, which will help further development
- More accuracy.
- Being able to print your own publicity material using a photo quality printer. The appearance of your business documents is important.

Technology is bringing increased productivity to small businesses in particular, and over half of small businesses now use latest technology to reach global markets.

Currently, improved productivity and reduced administration are seen as the major benefits of advanced technology. Technology also offers small businesses the opportunity to compete effectively with much larger companies, and in a market that is no longer restricted by geography.

The Internet

An easy and fast method of obtaining information is through the use of the Internet. There are number of search engines that could be a useful research medium for businesses of all types and sizes.

> **Tip:** *Google always seems to provide information you need very quickly, and currently it is the most widely used research medium worldwide.*

Furthermore, the use of global conferencing systems such as 'Usenet' enables people to conveniently communicate over the Internet. These conferences, referred to as 'newsgroups', deal with a wide variety of subjects.

'Mailing lists' are also useful for discussion on current issues and for obtaining advice and useful information from other people who are subscribed to the list. Knowledge sharing has become much easier now, and the Internet has brought people increasingly closer, despite the distance.

∞

Up and Running

Once your business is up and running, you will need to organise day-to-day management of your business efficiently. Good use of people, resources and technology will help you achieve just that and more. Now, is the time to focus your entrepreneurial spirit and evaluate where you need further assistance on improving brand awareness to drive your sales up. Seeking advice from a range of business experts, at every stage of your business is crucial.

Furthermore, if you are a business that needs to keep other people's data and records in your system, then under data protection law in the UK, you may have to provide details of how you handle personal data about staff or customers, for the data protection register. Therefore, you may be required to know the principles within your state/country that protect people's privacy with respect to the processing of personal data and how you store them, if appropriate to your business.

If you do not wish to keep customer information on documents and invoices and decide to destroy them, make sure that you dispose of them appropriately and safely. There are confidential waste services that take away and dispose of confidential waste safely.

Bookkeeping

Monitoring finances and processing and communication of financial information about economic entities in your business on a regular basis, is very important to assess profitability. Handling every day accounting accurately has to take priority, to recognise potential financial problems before they occur. Well-prepared financial data will be a key indicator as to how your business is currently performing. A good bookkeeping system does not necessarily have to be complicated. Depending on the size and nature of the business, you can decide how simple or complex a recording system you might need.

Spreadsheets are the most simple and commonly used bookkeeping system enjoyed by small business owners.

However, there are various especially designed accounting softwares available in the market these days, to handle more difficult financial data, if required.

There are compulsory book-keeping components utilised by anyone who is running a business. To manage such records you will have to have a cash book, balance sheet, wage books, sales records and purchase records.

It is worthwhile to keep all the records up to date and tidy, just in case someone wants to buy your business or an investor is interested in offering assistance for further development, or simply for your own easy reference.

- **Balance sheet** – indicates the financial position of the business at a defined date. This is considered the snap-shot of your business.

- **Profit and loss account** – is the most important account in all businesses. It covers all trading activities for any given accounting period. This summarises the company's income or turnover and the actual cost of those sales. This will also calculate the gross profits and net profits after taxes have been paid.

∞

Monitoring Business Performance

Regular monitoring of your business performance is especially important during an economic downturn.

Monitoring Performance

The key business elements such as suppliers, materials, efficiency, production, sales and revenue should also be incorporated into the business operation accurately and appropriately, while monitoring their performance, for a business to function at its best potential and achieve its optimum performance.

Business performance monitoring is an essential process that helps you measure whether your objectives are achieved at the end of a strategic stage as anticipated. Setting goals and objectives is an important activity that allows you to monitor this progress.

Measuring the performance is also important in identifying future opportunities and challenges for the business. What gets measured ensures visibility and control of every single important business activity, and consequently helps decision makers to take appropriate and timely decisions.

It is crucial for business owners to understand how well their business is progressing toward its goals. Therefore, it is necessary to implement a system to constantly monitor how the business is performing, in order to judge the 'success' against the business plan.

Quite often, variances occur between forecasts and actual performance in a business. This would be largely due to:

- a) **Fewer sales than expected** – a reduction in sales causes the gross profit to plummet.

- b) **Slower production than expected**

- c) **Using more materials than planned** – this will ultimately affect the total profit.

- d) **Debtors** – Overdue payments are an alarming matter for all small businesses. They are also one of the main reasons why small businesses fail too early. Therefore, it is important to negotiate the best possible terms for your business and your customers to minimise or eliminate potential bad debts altogether.

e) **Increase in cost of materials** – this will also result in a reduced profit margin.

f) **Wastage** – caused due to inefficient use of resources.

It is certainly important to keep a good track of the changes that occur within the business, assess how critical the above issues are and carefully monitor what their situation is, to be able to take preventative measures before they badly affect the overall business process. Hence, it is necessary to have a system in place to monitor the performance of all business activities periodically and employ essential strategies for growth.

Therefore, it is the responsibility of the owners to make sure that the key elements of their business are performing as they should, to secure a 'smooth ride'.

« CHAPTER – 5 »

Managing Cash Flow and Planning for Success

Cash flow is simply the money coming in and going out of your business at any moment in time. Cash flow forecasts will indicate how and when you except money to be received and paid out by your business. And it is essential to have a plan that will help you make your money work hard for you, now and in the future. A cash flow forecast is usually projected over a period of six or twelve months. These financial projections can also be used as a significant management decision-making tool for further development of your business.

Every business is different, but there is one thing all businesses must have in common, which is a good financial plan. A good financial plan can help you reach your goals much more quickly. Initially, when you are just beginning to operate, it is not necessary to spend money on complex accounting software, but you can use a simple Excel sheet or database table to monitor and organise the cash flow, and keep records of all your financial transactions in order.

However, as the business starts to grow you may need to utilise advanced accounting software to manage your finances more effectively. A general forecast has three equally important elements. Often, it is really good to keep an eye out for these basics to spot any financial irregularities, before they can affect the overall business operation. These important fundamental components that you should manage effectively are:

a) Cash in hand
b) Payments
c) Receipts

Monthly Totals

As a business owner it is essential to have an estimation of how much your approximate monthly totals will be. Keeping a total income and expenditure sheet in your office and ensuring that you have all licence fee and annual membership fees included in it is also vital, in order to calculate the actual totals. Additionally, it is necessary to maintain another report on actual total earnings and spending of the month separately, to assess the true financial capability of your business for each month.

These totals will help you identify varying or steady financial circumstances of your business end of every month, and assist you in creating more precise future financial plans.

Cash Flow Forecasts and Problems

Knowing how much money will be left in the business at the end of each month is extremely useful for any entrepreneur. Cash flow forecasts will give you an idea of what your cash flow will be, generally over the next twelve months. Be realistic, and account for things like seasonality and tax payments to get as precise as possible an evaluation of your future cash flow.

If at any point, your outgoings do not match your income, it is time to review your overall business and the strategies in place.

Leaving it until the last minute is not a great option. As soon as you realise the problems in your finances, it is essential to seek expert advice and also take immediate action such as trying to increase your overdraft or applying for loan or credit facilities with your bank to obtain some financial relief for these tough times. Also, it is worth making an assessment of your eligibility for government-backed schemes for small businesses or obtaining private financial backing, to move forward and avoid getting hit hard.

When your cash flow forecast is complete, you will need to keep records of how your business is actually performing. This information will be of great practical importance to you. Reviewing your current financial situation further and weighing up where your business stands at this moment is of great value.

Sometimes it is helpful to get expert financial advice to further assess the situation, and to get some important tips on how to protect the business from any potential dangers.

> *Tip: To enable you to run your business efficiently you must review your actual trading results against your original forecasts.*

∞

Financial Forecasts

In the early stages of your business, you may find that the income which you generate does not cover all your expenditure for the most part. Typically, this is because as a new business the initial income is generally slow at first. Also, there are setting up costs which are usually extremely high. However, before taking any decision on obtaining financial support, you should evaluate how committed you are to your business idea, and how confident you are that it will be successful. If you don't, running into unnecessary large debts will be inevitable.

For your business to remain profitable, overall revenue of the business should be higher than the outgoing costs. In simple terms, if your overall revenue is larger than the overall costs, then your business will hold more cash in 'the pot', making your business a decent profit.

In addition to being aware of your current finances, watching your future finance flow is also essential. If the flow of cash into your business ceases, then your business will not survive for very long. Such forecasts must be prepared on a realistic basis and you must be pessimistic rather than optimistic about them, thereby recognising the worst case scenario.

It is far better to work on the worst case and demonstrate that you can achieve a better performance even then.

If any part of the financial process is disrupted, you are most likely to encounter a shortage of cash. Also if your debtors are not paying you on time, do not allow them further credit until they have settled their debts.

It is a known fact that you never seem to have enough cash at the beginning of the business, no matter how well you are funded and how well you have organised the overall business tasks and operations.

It is absolutely crucial not to run into bad debt at the early stages of trading, to maintain a positive cash flow that will help you to eventually take the business to the next level.

Business owners must not underestimate the importance of maintaining a positive cash flow within their business at any given phase of trading to avoid running into huge debts.

Considering all the above, an efficient and a well thought-out financial plan is required, at least for the first year of trading to save your business from early closure.

Positive Cash Flow

Tip 1: You must maintain a tight control over your cash position. Do not allow your debtors to take advantage of you. They could cause your business to fail at an early stage.

Tip 2: Remember, profits don't mean anything if you don't hold that amount in cash. Until you receive cash from your customers, you haven't made a profit on the sale yet.

Tips to Improve Your Cash Flow

The following tips will help you manage your cash flow more effectively.

1) Don't tie up your cash and leave your business short, for day-to-day operation.
2) Make sure your customers pay you on time.
3) Pay your bills on time.
4) Spread costs over time.

Maintaining as smooth a flow of cash as possible on a daily basis will help you untangle any cash problems early and assist you in improving cash flow gradually, resulting in a profitable financial situation for the business.

More Hints:

- Use 'what-if' conditions.
   E.g. See what happens if sales are 10% higher or lower than your forecast
- Be cautious in the first few months of trading.
- Have 'cash reserves' to cover unexpected costs.

∞

Business Tax – The Basics

The general rule for all businesses is that, if you make a profit, you have to pay tax. And it is essential for every business owner to comply with the law and know what to pay, and when. By paying your taxes on time, you will be able to avoid penalties, fines and charges. It is key to know what your tax code is, because if you are on the wrong code, you may be paying too much or too little tax. If you are in doubt, seek professional advice from your accountant, bank or local authority.

It will always be useful to be up to date and knowledgeable about the general 'tax affairs' linked to your business if you are a serious entrepreneur.

Income Tax

It is a legal requirement to notify the tax office that you have commenced business. Tax requirements differ depending on the legal status of your business. Therefore, you should consider all requirements related to your business as soon as you start trading.

a) **Sole trader**: You are required to register as self-employed and pay personal income tax on all profits you make.

b) **In a partnership**: The partners are assessed separately and pay tax on their share of the profits.

c) **Company director**: You are also an employee and required to pay tax on the salary the company pays you.

Corporation Tax

If your business is a limited company you will need to pay corporation tax on your taxable profits.

National Insurance

If your business is not a limited company, you will need to register for National Insurance contributions.

Capital Gains Tax (CGT)

Capital Gains Tax is applied if you sell an asset for more than you paid for it.

Value Added Tax (VAT)

You must register to pay this tax on the sale of goods or services if your annual taxable turnover exceeds the registered limit.

If it is less, you may still choose to register; if you pay a lot of VAT on raw materials, then you can claim it back when you do so.

In any event, it is helpful to make a voluntary registration before your turnover reaches the limit.

Inheritance Tax (IHT)

If your business is a large part of your personal estate, you will need to plan for inheritance tax. Most business assets qualify for 100% business property relief, which means no IHT is due on them.

∞

Making Your Bank Work for You

Local business managers should understand your business and they may be able to advise you on ways to improve your cash flow.

In addition, they will be able to help with investment decisions that might increase your turnover significantly.

Building up Personal Savings

Whether you are running a business or not, it is important to establish personal cash reserves.

- ♦ Consider your personal savings as well as those of your business.

- ♦ Consider exposure to risk and involvement required before committing to an investment on a project, you are planning to undertake.

∞

The Books You Must Keep

All businesses are required to keep details of their transactions for current and future use and reference. The evidence of income and expenditure is usually referred to as the financial data of the business. Setting up a good bookkeeping system will assist you in accurate accounting, and to get the most out of your business while allowing you to keep an eye on the financial status at any financial period. This will also be helpful in recognising the business's financial position, after a year of trading.

You are legally obliged to keep your books and records for a certain period of time. Usually the requirement is to keep the records for at least six years. Business owners generally maintain printed copies or computer generated accounting packages to record these transactions. In this day and age it would be more appropriate to do it all on computer.

You must maintain several copies of these records in different locations to avoid losing important financial information due to natural disasters or theft.

The following books are typically used to keep information of the daily/weekly/monthly transactions of a business, in order to produce yearly accounts and generate taxable profits.

1) Cash Book

This can be used to record the income and expenditure of your business. In other words, all payments received and payments made must be noted and written down in your cash book. Writing a detailed record in this book will give you a clear picture of all the cash transactions of every single business day.

The end-of-month grand total of your cash book must match your bank balance, if you have done your sums right. It is crucial for you, as the business owner, to know your cash position at any given time.

This is especially critical as a new business, so that you can work out if your business is feasible. Also, this will enable business owners to be aware of early 'warning signs' of the cash position.

2) Petty Cash Book

The petty cash book records all the minor expenses. This might include spending on minor office supplies, postage, occasional travel costs, etc.

Usually, for all minor expenditure made, the receipts or proof of spending will be incorporated to balance out the transaction. It is also a good idea to have a separate book to prove any spending from petty cash that includes VAT details as well.

3) Purchase Book

This details the money you owe. This book records all transactions relating to credit purchases of goods. In other words, the records kept by a business of what it buys on credit each day will be maintained in this book. It is worth noting that cash purchases will not be entered here.

The purchase book is also known as the 'Invoice Journal' as it includes information on all invoices received. All these purchases you have made are recorded and calculated at the end of the month.

4) Sales Book

The sales book is to record details of people who owe you money. When you have sold goods to your customers a sales invoice is raised, and you can use this information to write up your sales book. When a sale is made, the original invoice will be given to your customer while you keep a copy for your records. Always remember to number your invoices and keep them in the right order, for your easy reference later.

Growing Your Business

If your business is showing the potential for growth, you may find it helpful to seek guidance of an expert or a mentor to take the business to the next level and keep moving forward. But, you should also not forget that there's no one set of rules for taking a small business to the next level.

Your business could potentially grow with time, through improved customer satisfaction and increased sales. For this, you must find the means to put a well-planned strategic management process to use.

Growth brings change, and when you are planning for growth of your business, you need to ask yourself the following questions.

  a) Are you in a strong financial position?
  b) Do you have the capital to expand?
  c) Are you covered, if things go wrong?

Consider taking the following steps to ensure that your start-up is on track for a prosperous year ahead.

1) Set Realistic Goals

Develop sensible objectives on what you want your business to achieve and a date to achieve it by. Setting up targets will give you something to work towards. Also make sure that those goals take your business where you want it to be.

2) Be Prepared to Take Risks

Decide how much risk you are prepared to take, almost immediately after starting your business. Early recognition of risks can help you to prevent many future business disasters. Conducting reviews on individual risks is crucial, but it is not a good idea to jump to conclusions without clearly knowing what the risk is about. The more you plan ahead, the better placed you will be, to face the unknown future. And never set plans that you are not comfortable with.

3) Get Expert Help

Getting things right from the beginning will help you create a solid foundation for your business. Also, an expert might be able to share his/her experiences with you, so that you will be able to avoid taking risky opportunities unknown to you.

Experts' views can make a real difference to your company's future. Therefore, talking to experts can help you get on the right track quickly and avoid unexpected failures.

4) The Key Actions

You need to understand where your business currently stands before you can start improving things. If things are progressing slowly, find out what is lacking and what areas you need to focus on, more. There are four simple key actions you can take into account, if you are seeking to move forward more effectively.

   a) Get more business from your existing customers.
   b) Get more business from new customers.
   c) Introduce new products and services to your existing customers.
   d) Introduce new products and services to new customers.

Nevertheless, there are pros and cons to each, but if you know what and who is involved, you will be in a better position to decide. Furthermore, you must learn the key benefits of the scalability of your business, as to whether your business can accommodate potential changes, and whether your business has sufficient room for expansion and improvement.

The objectives of a growing company face more transformation than an established one's do. However, for any business, it is worth having a global expansion plan in place for future use.

The winning formula is to constantly develop and enhance current products and services offered, while maintaining a continuous progression strategy.

Health Check Your Business

When your business is in the first few years of trading, it is essential to keep track of what profits you have made and what risks you are facing to plan better for future prospects.

Consider taking the following into account, in preparation for a safer and more productive business future.

- How much progress have you made?
- What are the most common causes of business failure in the first stages of your business and how could these have been avoided?
- Do you have a good idea of where you want to be in five years' time?
- Do you understand clearly who your customers are?
- Do you know the difference between turnover and net profit?
- Do you keep the right type of information systems?
- Is your pricing policy right?
- How well do you control your debts?
- How well do you manage your time?
- How efficiently do you use your equipment?
- Is your business strong enough to consider growth?

By answering the above questions honestly, you will able to assess your current business position accurately, to bring in new strategies to change it for the better.

Reasons for Business Failure

The general causes of failure are largely due to inexperience in managing and running a business. Observing the functions of each and every part of your business is equally important to prevent from early collapse. Poor management decisions also play a key role in early business failures. Therefore, a skilful manager should be able to prevent the business from unexpected closure by:

- Conducting frequent market research
- Managing the working capital effectively

- Monitoring financial performance wisely
- Reviewing targets on a regular basis
- Taking the right action and making decisions early
- Taking training in all areas when necessary
- Updating the business plan appropriately

Furthermore, some of the common reasons that a business might regrettably fail in the initial stages would be:

a) Bad debts
b) Increased competition
c) Lack of funding
d) Lack of sales

Therefore, it is crucial for business owners to understand these general reasons for why and how a business could fail, and utilise accurate strategies to constantly monitor how the business is performing. Also, employing the right people with the right attitude will be a sensible decision that a business leader can take to minimise potential risks.

∞

Planning for Success

Is There a Market for What I Offer?

An effective marketing plan will help you identify where your market is and what the current trends are. Talk to your family, friends, potential customers, experts and as many people as you can, about your marketing plans.

It is crucial for any business owner to find 'the gap' in the market or any potential great opportunities for what you are planning to offer. Ensure that you have the capacity to offer something different before your products and services are introduced to the emerging markets.

A customer-driven market approach is the way forward!.

Business Location

As referred to in Chapter 3, the right location is often critical to a business's success. Choosing the wrong location will have negative impact on profits, especially on a new business venture.

Setting up your business at home or in the city clearly has its own advantages and disadvantages. For businesses in some sectors, location really is important, especially if you are in the retail or food business. The correct location is key to successful operation and overall growth for these businesses.

Knowing what suits you the most and making the right decision, is what matters.

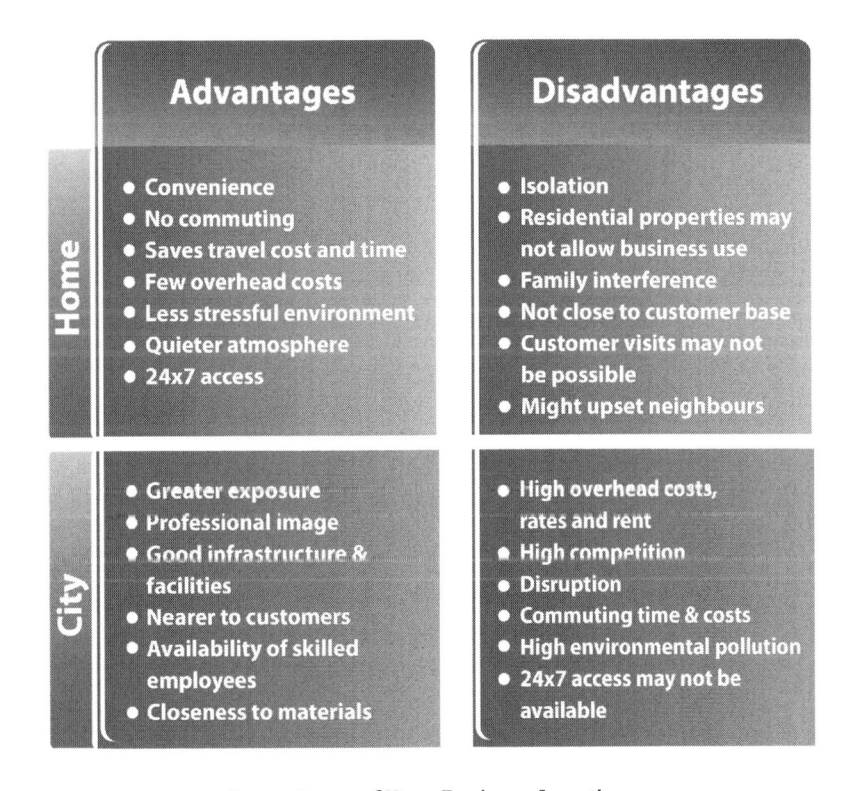

	Advantages	Disadvantages
Home	• Convenience • No commuting • Saves travel cost and time • Few overhead costs • Less stressful environment • Quieter atmosphere • 24x7 access	• Isolation • Residential properties may not allow business use • Family interference • Not close to customer base • Customer visits may not be possible • Might upset neighbours
City	• Greater exposure • Professional image • Good infrastructure & facilities • Nearer to customers • Availability of skilled employees • Closeness to materials	• High overhead costs, rates and rent • High competition • Disruption • Commuting time & costs • High environmental pollution • 24x7 access may not be available

Importance of Your Business Location

Therefore, where to locate your business is a crucial decision for many entrepreneurs. It is worth taking note of the advantages and disadvantages that 'home' and locations in the 'city' have to offer, when making this all-important decision. And it is critically important to choose the 'RIGHT' location for your business carefully, if you are planning for success.

However, well-known businesses and brands in the market don't usually get affected by wrong positioning. In fact, people tend to buy from them, despite the location in which they are based. However, unfortunately the businesses that are new to the market don't have this advantage until they make a name for themselves.

You should also consider company needs, customer needs and employee needs when deciding on your business location.

Your Competitors

Knowing what your direct competitors are doing and learning about their strengths and weaknesses is imperative for any business that aspires to do well. Such information will make it easier for you to be aware of what you are up against in the market, from the early days of the business.

When analysing your competition, you must know what to look for, where to stop and when to draw the line.

Monitoring the way your competitors do business and having a clear and precise understanding of how they operate, what resources they use effectively, their successful marketing strategies, involvement of experts, their acceptance and perception within the society, etc are of great value to anyone starting on their own.

Do you have a 'USP'?

Before you can begin to sell your product or service to anyone else, you have to sell yourself on it. Developing a USP begins with your target audience, and to do that you have to make a stand for something.

Advertise, promote and make people aware about your Unique Selling Point very frequently. Create 'the need' for customers to buy from you, and not someone else or your competitor.

However, if you sell the same or similar products or services as everyone else in the market, make sure that your USP has something more to offer. Avoid just competing on price alone. Regularly reflect, review and improve on quality, efficient service and customer care in the products and services you are planning to sell.

How to Make a Profit?

When setting your prices for your products and services, there are a number of basics that you must take into account. Firstly, you should be able to work out your initial pricing by considering:

a) Household and personal overheads
b) Business overheads and costs

While keeping an eye on the above costs, you must review the following and recognise their importance when setting up pricing.

c) Develop your products and services often
d) Emphasise the differences between what you and your competitors offer, and justify the price
e) Reduction of your costs

Once you have analysed your general costs and possible improvement and development plans for what you are planning to offer, then you will be able to set reasonable pricing for your products and services. If the gap between your income and costs is higher, then clearly your business will yield great profit margins. And remember you have to work hard for this to happen. Nothing comes easy, especially for start-ups.

How Do You Promote Your Business?

The promotional activities you are planning to carry out should be able to generate a desire for potential buyers to purchase from you.

Whatever your business is, word-of-mouth referrals are certainly likely to be one of the most effective marketing tools in the current economic climate. And it is your job to try your best to:

- Offer the best product and service possible.
- Build trustful long-term connections with your customers.
- Sort out problems and offer quick solutions.
- Be transparent, passing on information clearly and without delay.

Generally, happy customers tend to talk about your business and they don't hesitate to share their stories with others. And you must become 'that business' that they talk about. Usually, a business owner's personal life becomes his/her public life. Which is why you need to be careful what you put on social media. However you must remember that your friends in social media networks could eventually become a customer.

If you believe you have attractive solutions to the questions below and can support or agree with the statements, you will know how best to promote your products or services, potentially better than your competitor will.

a) What features of your business stand out and offer a better deal?

b) Your advertising campaign must be an appealing one. And your advert must 'shout-out' who you are and what you sell. Make it the 'most talked' about advert of the day/week.

c) What advertising mediums are available to you? Are they producing the outcome you would like?

d) Make sure you sell exactly what you say on your adverts. Deliver what is promised. Also make sure that you keep in line with the Advertising Standards Code of Practice. Seek advice from your local Trading Standards Office for further information.

e) Remember the power of pictures and videos. They capture people's hearts.

f) Think differently. Think of creative ways of getting attention. Are you doing everything you can to make your product or service well known?

g) Work on PR. What activities could you organise to make people remember you?

h) Don't forget to get feedback from new customers. Measure the success. Use diverse advertising platforms and change the message you put across to your customers accordingly.

Work out what promotional activities suit you the best. Let your creative mind play. Draw a picture, write a story, come up with new ideas and get noticed if you want to succeed in your promotional efforts.

« CHAPTER – 6 »

Getting Ready for Marketing

Marketing is one of the key areas that demands attention from any business owner who is ambitious and determined to do well. Marketing generally involves communicating to the marketplace that you have a product or service to offer. Without a smart and resourceful marketing plan in place, your efforts to attract customers will be tricky.

Every business must make sure that its products and services meet customer needs better than its competitors. Therefore, understanding your customers and their needs effectively and fast is essential, while employing the right marketing medium to reach them.

Being 'market ready' simply means, getting every marketing idea and plan in place. A marketing strategy that can respond to changes in market trends and customer demands is one that your business should be considering incorporating into its marketing plan.

Once you have implemented your marketing strategies, it is important to monitor their effectiveness, efficiency and performance, to evaluate their success. A great marketing plan is all about making sure that the customers choose you over your competitor, and when this is achieved, the rest will follow.

∞

Marketing Plan

While working hard to reach new customers, you also need to make sure that you are not neglecting existing customers' demands. It is vital to keep improving your marketing efforts and watch your competition quite regularly. Setting out clear objectives and ensuring that your marketing plans become a reality is valuable. Also, you must not overlook adopting well-researched strategies to have a much better chance of building long-term, profitable relationships with your existing customer base, which is important for anyone running a business.

It doesn't matter what type of promotional activity you have in mind for your business, you must set up clear goals for each and every marketing campaign, to analyse their success. And it is important to ensure that you allow the promotional techniques you are using sufficient time to work. Marketing plans don't usually work overnight. The customers need time to make their decision to buy or not to buy from you.

What matters here, is to have a solid marketing strategy in place, to carry out tasks from analysing the market situation and market segments to recommending alternatives to evaluating the implications, in order to measure up the success of every single marketing effort taken.

∞

Writing a Marketing Plan

The secret to successful marketing is a well-written marketing plan. Your marketing plan needs to reflect the resources you have put into it, such as money, time and skills to measure the results. Then, carrying out a SWOT analysis and focusing on the Strengths, Weaknesses, Opportunities and Threats of your business is required. Also identify what you are aiming to achieve at the end of each marketing project.

Market Research and Reports

Needless to say, it is so important to understand your target market accurately, how to sell to your customers effectively, how to compete with other suppliers, how to improve productivity and find better solutions and how to spot new opportunities.

In this highly competitive market place, being dedicated to improving your knowledge by carrying out surveys, discussions and investigating customer attitudes, changing behaviours and trends is equally valuable for every marketing manager and his/her team. Performing comprehensive market research is essential for a business to survive in today's aggressive marketplace.

Additionally, it will be useful for business owners to keep all research material, data and information recorded for future use and further research.

These reports of market research will be an invaluable source of information for business development and also for potential entrepreneurs, all those who wish to become self-employed or even for experts in the field.

Moreover, such valuable information on market research and reports could also be made available for interested individuals and companies to purchase to improve their knowhow.

Forecast and Plan Your Sales

Good sales forecasts on a great sales plan can help you escape unexpected cash flow problems and manage your financing needs more effectively. A well thought-out sales forecast is key to increasing the sales of businesses of any size. With a sensible sales prediction, you will be able to spot opportunities more quickly, and identify problems and do something about them before it is too late. A great sales plan and realistic forecast will allow you to spend more time improving your business, and eliminating problems that may occur in the future.

Also, a well-planned sales forecast will allow you to organise an effective marketing plan accordingly.

Using the Internet

A marketing plan must accompany strategies of Internet marketing, and demonstrate how small business owners can take effective advantage of them. Internet marketing involves the use of digital media to inform people of your presence in the market.

A successful business is based on professionalism, expert service and great after-sales care. A lot of these could be achieved by appropriate use of the Internet and its resources. Using Internet resources can also reduce or eliminate the need for using the traditional postal service and all of the costs associated with it.

Today, more and more people are using Internet technology to shop online. Hence, it is important for your business to have a clear presence on the Internet through social media, online business networks, Twitter, Facebook, online advertisements, etc.

Therefore, if you intend to grow your business fast, the Internet has a large part to play in your marketing plan.

However, even just putting too much information on, even if it's not offensive, is probably not a good idea.

As previously mentioned in Chapter 5, when you have a business you need to be careful about what personal information you put on social media, as compromising details and photos could damage the reputation of your business.

The Website

An important component that should be included in your marketing plan is the 'Company Website'. The right website can make all the difference to your sales margins.

A professionally designed website can accurately highlight the benefits of products and services you offer, and clearly reflect what your business is all about. With the current popularity of the Internet, many consumers nowadays tend to check a company's website before choosing to do business with them or buying from them. Hence, making sure your website is mobile friendly and compatible with the latest web browsers is the key. Also, the need for any firm to have a website for any firm has become more crucial than ever before, for small businesses in particular, considering their costs are extremely high at the entry level. A well-designed website will bring your business a good image and a solid customer base.

Using technology to get your website to the top of the search engines will clearly improve your visibility on the Internet. Integrating social media networks such as Facebook and Twitter on-to your website is a smart way of keeping your customers engaged, while being able to monitor their behaviours and identify latest trends. Including testimonials on your website is a smart way of revealing your relationship to potential buyers as well.

However, it is crucial to avoid using a lot of graphics or heavy pictures on your website that take a long time to load, as your customers may not want to wait for more than five seconds for the website and its pages to load.

Your website is your image on the web! And it is worth keeping in mind that a website can boost or damage the image of any business within a short period of time.

So be cautious, and don't underestimate the power of your 'company website', what it has to offer and what it can do to make or break a deal.

Future Planning

It is a sensible decision for any business owner to put a long-term marketing plan in place. This will often help you work out the current strategies, analyse changes and refine the plans, as and when necessary, to win new business.

∞

Know Your Customers

However good your product or service is, people will not buy from you if they don't want it or believe they don't need it. Therefore, it is essential to recognise what it is your customers actually want, and how often they need it. Understanding customer needs is important to every business aiming to accomplish its goals. If you think that implementing a comprehensive customer service plan is too expensive, take your time to consider the potential profits and growth that are lost without one.

If you are a service provider, always insist on providing your service under an agreed contract. Carry out research to find out legal constraints related to your service. Consult your legal advisor for further information if necessary.

The primary objective of every business should be to provide the best product and service possible to its customers, or else its business journey is highly likely to be short-lived.

Getting to Know Your Customers

The first step in the book of marketing is to understand who your customers are and how your product or service will benefit them.

Moreover, it would be incredibly beneficial for anyone running a business to distinguish their best customers, establish how to reach them effectively, and have a clear understanding about their competitors.

Your Best Customers

Up to 80% of your income is likely to come from 20% of your customers. Therefore, it is important to keep existing customers happy, by ensuring that you can accommodate their changing needs and perspectives at any given time. Recognise what each customer is worth to your business.

It is a proven fact that the best way to increase customer loyalty is through improved customer service.

Customer loyalty is the solution to customer retention.

Reach Your Customers Effectively

Every business needs customers to survive and thrive. Selecting the right medium to sell to them is an important decision. Clearly, the more sales channels you use, the more people you can reach. But remember, each channel will add to your costs.

Therefore, selecting the right marketing mediums and using them to the best advantage, is the particularly crucial decision that a marketing manager has to make.

If your target customers are the youth then remember that they spend more time on social media channels and the Internet. Aim your promotional activities to appear, where the potential customers may see you the most. Having a clear picture about the suitable market segments for your business would be an added advantage here.

Today, more and more customers buy online. Therefore, making sure your business is visible on the Internet and utilising user-friendly platforms is crucial to improve sales potential.

Understanding Your Competitors

To truly understand the strengths of your own business and your position in the market, you must have a sound understanding of your competition, and see how your business compares to your competition by carrying out intensive market research.

Knowing who your competitors are and what they sell will help you find your USP, enable you to set your prices competitively and subsequently improve on performance.

Understanding your competition clearly means a greater opportunity to supply a product or service that fills a unique gap in the market. However, it is not a good idea to attempt everything that your competitors do.

What is right for your competitor may not be right for you.

Hence, your policy always should be to do what you are good at, and offer the best possible product or service to your customers, at the right time and price.

Threats posed by new entrants to the market are another common issue faced by small business owners.

Preparing for change, the ability to adapt to those changes and being able move past challenges, are critical success factors for all budding entrepreneurs.

> *Tip: Use price as an effective marketing tool. Be in the right place, at the right time, with the right quality and quantity of products and services, if you are planning to grow.*

Customer-led Marketing

The crucial part of customer-led marketing is determining the customer category you want to reach, planning all your activities around them, and offering products and services that work better for them.

Consumers' Impact on Your Business

Customer-led marketing is mainly focused around the feedback of your valued customers and more importantly, what they say to potential customers about you. Remember, there is no other marketing method as powerful as word of mouth and referrals coming from your existing customer base.

The voice of your customer must be the core of your business and your important business decisions.

Good consumer influence will bring positive growth to your business more quickly than any other marketing method in use.

A great testimonial from a happy customer can put across your 'good' image to others. Sharing a customer's good experience regarding your products or services will prove your credibility for new customers in particular, and encourage them to approach you. A good brand image is invaluable for a start-up to make its mark in the competitive business environment.

Tip: Put your customer first !

The Internet's Dominance

It is already proven that clever use of the Internet can drive customer-led marketing to positively influence business growth. Your business must be all about conversation and building long-term relationships. These days, the Internet has given people and businesses a greater voice.

Therefore, more voices are heard, more information is exchanged and more common interests are shared, as a result of the easy accessibility of the Internet.

As for business owners, the marketing has become an engaging two-way street. The online conversations of your customers create a greater chance of ensuring their return. Satisfied customers will do the marketing for you. They will send people to your website and to your business.

Therefore, it's time to begin the conversation online!

The Social Media Influence

Today, social media has a powerful say and a major influence on what we do and how we do things. Currently, networking on social media has never been easier or more affordable with the popularity of high speed broadband.

The social media networks available through the Internet will help discover your customers' view-point on what you offer, what they are most likely to buy, and changing market trends, faster than ever before.

If you have a strong relationship with your existing customers you can ask them to share your information on your website, Facebook page, share promotional emails, e-flyers and comment on your products and services, to improve awareness.

A satisfied customer might be willing to spread the word about having a good experience with you. Turn your service into a long-term relationship.

Make friends, make sales.

So, it is time to approach your social media audience, engage them in conversation and make a sale!

Improving Customer Loyalty

It is challenging for any company to retain their customers for as long as they can. The ability to retain customers through business insight can often determine the success or failure of a business. It is a well-known fact that getting new customers costs much more than retaining the ones who have already built up relationships and done business with you. Consistently finding ways to improving customer relationships will save your business a lot of time, effort and money, eventually saving the overall business from collapse.

Key Components for Customer Retention

It has been established that the time, effort and cost of gaining a new customer is far greater than that of retaining an existing one. In fact, attracting a new customer can cost you five times that of keeping an existing one. This information alone explains the significant value of your existing customer.

Therefore, measuring up the key ingredients that you currently possess, and identifying where your business and services currently stand, is extremely useful to improving customer loyalty and to enabling your business to thrive in this highly competitive market.

Check if your business demonstrates the following key features that are incredibly important for growing a sustainable business. Ultimately, customer retention has been proven to create long-term success.

How responsive are you, as a business? It's time for a quick review....

1) Quality

Get feedback from your customers and analyse the weaknesses of your service and products more often. At the same time, it is also important to know your strengths and what you do well to emphasise those good qualities. All the feedback you get, whether negative or positive will help you to continuously improve quality and is useful for training purposes. Speak to your customers after a sale and get their views, and hear how they feel about the product or service offered.

Make sure your customers are satisfied with you first, to be able to build a strong long-term association with them. Understand customer needs and ensure that what you offer is what customers really want. In the meantime, use your resources effectively to reduce customer waiting times and price by building up on quality and this should lead to profits in the long run.

2) Responsiveness

Understand your customers' urgency. Provide them with trouble-free access to services and products they may need, as quickly as possible.

Be responsive to, and responsible for, the events happening inside your boundary line and sometimes even outside of your limits, to provide a far broader service, as this might be the element that differentiates you from your competition.

Make the right decisions and respond to emails or letters swiftly. If a customer makes a complaint it is ideal to put it straight through to the person who can resolve the matter as soon as possible.

3) Reliability

Reliability brings new opportunities. Assure your customers that they will receive the same top quality service or product every time they do business with you.

Simple acts such as answering the phone or responding to an email efficiently can make a positive impact on your business and customers will rely on you to offer a good service or product as promised.

The ability to be reliable, dependable, and trustworthy is important for the progression of any company. This indicates the degree of honesty and quality of the business, and it will ultimately be the deciding factor in whether your consumers are prepared to make a long-term commitment with you.

4) Empathy

As a business, the ability to understand your customer is essential to providing an excellent customer experience. If a customer is excited about your products or services, share that excitement with them. Listen to them and establish a rapport with them. Give your customers the opportunity and time to explore the product or service. Do not rush for a sale.

Understanding your customers, showing you really care and making them feel valued, will improve your potential of being the best in the market. And those customers will stick with you for a long time to come.

5) Credibility

A credible business must be able to deliver exactly what they say they will deliver, every time they make a sale. Businesses that are credible have simple and straightforward business models. Being honest is important to increasing customer numbers. Be as open as possible about the information you provide, and the attitude that you convey to your buyers.

Providing and enhancing value consistently, will constantly remind your customers of the great products and services you are offering them, and remind them of how you differ from your competitors. Do something additional, and make them aware of it, and make them remember you.

Such activities will make you stand out. If you cannot take an extra step or go beyond the boundary line, do let the customers know your limitations well in advance.

You must build credibility by building trust!

6) Trust

You must create a sense of customer belonging to build trust. The same rule applies to your employees. Treat your employees as internal customers because securing their trust and loyalty is important for business success. Your employees will treat customers exactly the way you treat them. Involve your team in company decision making. You must not forget that your employees reflect the attitude of your business. They are, simply put, the ambassadors of the business.

Invite both customers and employees to take part in development strategies and improvement efforts within the business. Make good use of their feedback. Keep employees informed about every bit of your business and trust them to do their jobs well.

Also keep your customers informed about what your latest offers and newest products are, and listen to what they have to say. Value their contribution. Make them a part of your business. Consider both your employees and consumers as partners of your business. Build their trust from the moment you take them on board. This is the way forward for building long-term commitment.

7) Expertise

To be the expert in the market, you must train your people continually. Define how and where your staff wish to extend knowledge and experience.

Organise training programmes to build on expertise, skills and area of interest, which are critical to your company's development. Focus on improving your employees' communication skills, technical knowledge, customer service skills and effectiveness at solving problems. You must be able to hire good people to work for you, and select frontline employees based on intelligence, not just skills.

Hire cheerful personalities and people with great attitudes. One bad attitude is more than enough to damage your business's reputation. Continuously motivate, praise and reward your team's good performance. Make them feel appreciated.

Value and respect everyone's opinion. Make combined business decisions and build a sense of belonging with your business. Offer your customers access to their expert knowledge and a diverse range of information.

It is ideal to have a system in place to enhance employee knowledge, their productivity and to reward them for great performance. Provide constant guidance for your employees to change for the better. Get regular feedback.

You should evaluate whether you are in possession of the above attributes if you are looking to improve customer loyalty and long-term relationships.

∞

Further into Marketing

The decision as to how much to spend on marketing will depend on the size and type of business you are in. Inevitably, some marketing methods will work better than others. You can find out what works better only by trying.

Concentrate more on the marketing strategies that provide the best return on investment. However, being able to discover such strategies is the crucial part.

It is a good idea to spend more time on small promotional activities first, such as giving away freebies and discounts, as a new business, before moving into more costly activities.

However, as your business grows bigger and holds more working capital, you will be able to invest in marketing activities that require considerable amounts of funds that will provide your business with greater exposure.

Try the following marketing methods to boost your sales, and identify which of them is best for your business.

Direct Marketing

Direct mail, leaflet drops, telemarketing and email marketing falls into this category. These methods allow you to target customers with greater accuracy than any other method.

Trade Shows and Exhibitions

Trade shows and exhibitions allow businesses to market their products and services, reach potential customers and generate new leads. These shows also give visitors the chance to find out more about your products and services, and get a good view of, and feel about them, in person. Trade shows and exhibitions also provide businesses with the opportunity to meet people, make contacts and exchange ideas, which is an extremely useful opening for small businesses in particular.

Business Network Meetings

This will be a great opportunity to meet people and even consider opportunities on how small businesses can work together for a better future.

This low cost marketing method has become a very popular medium of promotion today. Being a regular member of business networking groups in your area, and meeting local business contacts to get local knowledge, is extremely useful, at any stage of your business journey.

Social Media Networks

In the current market 80% of your customers are on social media networks and it is easy to reach them via social media these days. Therefore, there's a very good chance of meeting your future consumers there. Social media platforms are very popular networking mediums of today, and they keep changing all the time.

These social networks help you build social relations among people who share interests, activities or real-life experiences. And this is a useful way of recognising potential customer trends. Most importantly, these are free marketing tools that can deliver a prompt message to the market your business operates in.

Obtaining such information via these platforms will be beneficial for business owners in reaching their target market. Satisfied customers are more likely to share your information on social media, and these platforms will be invaluable for new business owners. However, you must also be aware that there is the potential to do a business a lot of damage if a dissatisfied customer posts on them.

Social media is one of the most effective marketing tools a small business owner can use and it gives you the option to select which devices that you want to go live with your advert: Desktop, Laptop, or Mobile. You can plan your advert to get the maximum productivity and visibility by adjusting the campaign's targeted audience. Setting up tracking that can show important metrics such as site visits, purchases, and other actions will be helpful too. And by using pictures and fresh, more engaging content will improve campaign performance. However, your budget must reflect how much a visitor to your website/facebook page/etc is worth to your business.

Tip: Every happy customer is a marketing tool.

As a business owner or someone who is hoping to start their own business soon, it would be helpful to recognise how the above marketing methods can identify consumer behaviour and how such methods can drive revenue. Therefore, smart use of marketing strategies, and when and where to use them, are essential to secure a profitable and stable position in the current market.

Marketing vs. Advertising – The Difference

People often confuse marketing with advertising. While both are important promotional activities, they are very different. But both offer extremely powerful methods of publicity for almost any type of business.

Marketing: is orderly planning, organising and executing of a variety of business promotional activities that bring together buyers and sellers. These activities establish the presence of the seller in the market, by introducing its products or services to the potential buyer. Marketing is a much bigger process than advertising that involves intensive research and effort.

Advertising: is utilising public announcements with a persuasive message by a business about the products or services it offers, aiming at the existing and potential customers, by using selected media. These are often paid placements and it is the largest expense of all activities.

Therefore, advertising can be considered as only just one element of the entire marketing plan. What is crucial for anyone running a business is their ability to identify the most appropriate marketing method(s) for their business, and how to execute those methods as effectively as possible to yield the best outcome.

« CHAPTER – 7 »

Advertising Your Business

It is not easy to get people talking about your business. With a bit of creativity and effort, there are a number of ways to promote your business and get people talking. In order for your business to become a known brand in the market, it is essential to have some 'smart' advertising strategies in place.

Is Advertising Really Essential?

Advertising is just one of the many elements in the marketing plan. Currently, there are many free advertising tools and cost-effective ways of advertising available for small businesses. Some of them are completely free to implement. It is really not necessary to spend a lot of money on advertising when some of the best opportunities are free.

However, it is also important to understand that there are advertising options available in the market that will cost you a fortune as well.

And it is challenging for any owner to pick the best advertising method and medium for their business, especially when starting out. In this highly competitive world of business, advertising is the central platform to get people talking. But you should not depend on advertising methods alone to bring in sales.

Yet, is advertising really essential? Every expert thinks it is!

The marketing experts recommend the following seven fundamental principles for developing a successful advertising plan.

1) The Headline

The headline is the most important element of your advert. The headline needs to grab people's attention, the moment they see it. The idea of the headline is not to sell your product or service, but just to get people to read your advert, first. Be adventurous and creative with your headlines. Test different versions to see what works best. Use short, simple and easy to understand headlines.

Create your headline, and get 'heads' turning.

2) Stress the Benefits

One of the principles of advertising is to reveal the benefits in order to draw attention to your products or services. Therefore, your advert needs to be a personal communication tool to the person hearing, reading, or seeing it. By highlighting the benefits, it repeatedly reinforces the idea that your products or services are exactly what the customer has been looking for.

If your customer is aware of the good value offered by you, then there is a great chance of him/her passing on the message and recommending your service or product to other likely consumers and markets, without any hesitation. However, the other side of this is that, if your customer finds out the good value offered by you is not good enough, there is the great danger of him/her damaging your business's image. But, this should not put you off emphasising the advantages of what you offer and being honest about them.

3) Formula of AIDA

Good use of AIDA has proven to be a winning formula in adverting. Try incorporating these ideas in your advertising plan, if you are seeking to attract your customers' interest.

- **A**ttention – Grab the consumer's attention with your headline.
- **I**nterest – Generate an interest in the product or service you offer.
- **D**esire – Transfer the consumer's interest into an aspiration strong enough to make a purchase.
- **A**ction – Call to action. Tell people precisely what to do and how to take action after seeing your message.

4) Paying for Your Advert

Most advertising rates are generally high, but there's always an opportunity to negotiate the price. If you are a small business, you will sometimes be able to pay 20 or 30% less for your advert and turn an unprofitable advert into a successful one. You must not forget that most publications have deadlines to meet. The closer to the deadline you can get, the better it is if you want to grab a bargain. Sales teams become desperate to fill these spaces left and you might be able to grab a good deal on them.

In such situations, it is worth putting your negotiation skills into practice for a good bargain or upgrade. However, there is an element of risk attached to these bargains, when publications run out of spaces towards the end.

Prices for featuring an advert may vary depending on the category, word count, pictures and duration you choose to advertise for. Deciding what works best for you is essential.

And it is your responsibility to provide all the relevant information to the advertising media before your advert can go live.

5) Your Competition

It is important to remember not to advertise on various forms of media just because your competitors are doing so.

Don't assume that all your competitors' adverts are producing great results. Their adverts are more likely to be there because everyone else has advertised, and most of them might not know whether their advertising is effective and producing the expected results or not.

In this instance, it is not a good idea to go with the market flow. However, deciding on the best medium suitable for your business, without spending large amounts of money unnecessarily, is tricky. It is also not ideal to follow the methods that other popular businesses employ, especially if you are a small business or start-up, as such methods will not be the most 'favourable' for your business. It is very easy to lose track of your finances, when it comes to advertising.

In summary, you always need to be vigilant where and what you are spending your money on.

6) The Best Positioning for Your Advert

This applies if you are advertising in a newspaper or magazine. When you read a magazine, newspaper or journal, etc, your eyes are more drawn to the right hand page. And there is a better chance of people seeing your advert if it is on the right hand page. This concept has been tested again and again. Therefore, the best place for similar media is the 'right'.

However, advertisements that appear on the left hand page will cost you less, because it is a known fact that less people will see it. Hence, if you are on a very tight budget, but still want to take a chance and get some exposure, then choosing to advertise on the 'left' is the right option.

So do not be tempted. Spend your marketing budget wisely, productively and effectively to reap the rewards.

• Self - Employment – The Secret to Success •

Advertising Your Business

7) Is Your Advert Working?

This applies to any type of advertising method you are currently using to promote your business.

It doesn't matter where your advertisement is running, whether in newspapers, magazines, on billboards, posters, on radio, television, etc, if they are not working, simply stop running them before wasting more money!

It is also important to test all of your advertising results every time an advert expires. Otherwise, you are not going to find out if the advert has been fruitful or not.

It would be useful for anyone running a business to know how many people responded and how many of them were converted into a sale, thereby instantly learning how profitable the advert has been, and deciding whether to continue or discontinue the advert, or to employ an entirely different advertising plan.

Also, you must constantly analyse the figures and graphical representations in your marketing table, to get a clear idea of how effective your adverts have been.

By measuring these responses that you have received against the cost, and by deriving from the facts approximately how much you spend on a favourable new customer, you will be able to decide whether the advert is worth the hard work or not.

Any business can reap rewards from using the above rules and using these rules effectively and appropriately in the right place.

And the choice is yours!

∞

The Secrets of Successful Advertising

By now, you must know what you are selling, what type of people you will sell to, and why they will buy from you. By sticking to the advice and strategies below, you will be able to produce an effective advertising campaign for your audience and find success from it.

More About Advertising

Advertising in general is getting the word out about what you do as a business. Advertising comprises posting an advert in mediums such as newspapers, direct mail, billboards, television, radio, the Internet, etc. Every business owner is aware that advertising is the largest cost of most marketing plans and that they have to plan the budget wisely to get their money's worth.

Grabbing your prospective customers' attention and keeping them interested, while telling them how you can help them, and inspiring them to buy from you, is successful advertising.

This approach helps most small businesses to grow at a rapid and steady pace. Using attention-grabbing words like these can make all the difference to ensuring your advert is a success:

- "best"
- "effective"
- "free free free"
- "excellence"
- "expert"
- "specialist"

Therefore, when you can only afford a little quarter page advert, you have to do everything you can to make it as effective as possible by utilising the above 'all-important' words appropriately.

Make the most of what is available to you such as budget, skills, creativity, media and time to produce the best advert achievable to yield impressive results.

Make sure your advertisement has been created in such a way that it is:

a) **Aggressive** – Your advert must motivate the potential consumer to buy from you rather than just be "aware". However, it is also important that your advert does not make the buyer feel he/she is being pushed for a sale.

b) **Generating Hot Leads** – Your ad needs to include a way for people to contact you and leave their details as part of the "call to action". At the end of the promotion, you should have the name, address, phone number and email address of people thinking about using your product or service at a future date. The next step is to contact them and tell them about the benefits of your product or service, how different you are from your competition, and create an opportunity for a sale.

c) **Traceable** – By counting the number of leads who responded to your advert, you can work out the cost-per-lead, which serves as a benchmark for your next advertising campaign. By assessing these results, you should be able to decide if the advert has been successful or not.

Measuring the effectiveness of your advertising campaign will usually help businesses to avoid costly mistakes in the future, to review and bring about new and efficient strategies.

Evaluating success and suggesting alternative strategies to increase efficiency is important to increase profitability. However, it is important to understand that measurable growth in sales may not be immediately forthcoming and your business will not be transformed overnight.

Hitting the Target

When planning your advertising campaign, it is crucial to make sure that the message you are trying to express and the response you want to generate are just right.

Placing your advert in a medium that your prospective customers will see or hear will be the next key decision. Find out if you have hit the target, by looking into how effective your advert has been by evaluating the responses, analysing sales you have made, and asking your customers where they heard about you.

Advertising on a Low Budget

If your advertising budget is limited, which it usually is at the start, you will still have plenty of free or low budget advertising options available in the current media. Therefore, it is essential for business owners to develop their awareness by finding out what is available for them and where. However, if a generous advertising budget is available to you, organising a large marketing promotion on the right channel will bring far greater results.

Take into consideration these ideas, if you are on a low advertising budget, but you really shouldn't be dependent on only one option, out of many.

Ideally, you could use a combination of strategies such as:

a) Advertise on other people's websites
b) Advertise in shop windows
c) Distribute leaflets
d) Get free editorial space in local newspapers
e) Impress customers by giving them something free with their first purchase
f) Place a small advertisement in your local paper
g) Set up a website
h) Sponsor a local team or event; this needn't be an overly expensive option
i) Use social media networks effectively

Remember, these methods can even give you similar results to your 'big-budget' competitors, at a fraction of the cost.

The best way to know if this is true is only by trying the above advertising methods, and measuring the end result.

Tip: Word-of-mouth referral is beyond price.

∞

Where Does Advertising Go Wrong?

There is plenty that can go wrong with advertising especially if you are starting out.

Therefore, it is important to consider the following main reasons why and how your advertising activities could go wrong. If you are not aware of these or you do not pay enough attention to them, or completely disregard them, you will later regret wasting the limited finances you might have.

All your efforts will go to waste if your advertisement is:

1) Aimed at the wrong people
2) Cluttered and confusing
3) Featured in only one advertising medium
4) Featured in the wrong medium
5) Seen at the wrong time
6) Not giving the customer a motive to act instantly
7) Not making your product or service appealing enough
8) Not well planned
9) Not noticeable or doesn't stand out
10) Stopped before the advertising can work, or not repeated

Also it is extremely important not to include information that is false, misleading or harmful anywhere in your advert.

By learning and understanding these most common advertising mistakes in advance, you will be able to avoid such errors, and produce an advert that proves to be successful.

∞

Designing Your Advertisement

Writing and designing an attention-grabbing advertisement is, in fact, skilled work. That is why there's a regular need and demand for a professional to get the advert designed for you.

A well-designed advert has more possibilities for attracting potential buyers and the ability to transfer their interest into a sale than a poorly designed one. It is worth taking note of different styles, sizes and types of adverts used by current business ventures and getting your advert created appropriately.

Furthermore, all the advertising and promotional materials you are hoping to use must be fair, clear and not give out misleading information to the viewers. Expressing your message clearly in plain language and avoiding using technical or legal language wherever possible is also vital. Additionally, explaining your products and services and their terms and conditions clearly on the advert should also not be ignored.

Smart Advertising

The basics of smart adverting will be to include the following simple concepts in all your promotional activities:

- ♦ Opening with a question or statement
- ♦ Words and graphics to help the customer make a decision
- ♦ Encouraging the customer to contact you now (the call to action)

The way that businesses advertise their products and services nowadays is becoming 'smarter' by the day. Therefore, all businesses, new and old, must adapt these 'smart and creative' techniques of advertising, rather than disregarding them completely, if they are aiming for success.

The Right Medium for Your Advertising

Today, there are a wide variety of advertising methods commonly used by companies of different types and sizes. Each of the following advertising methods has its own advantages and features. Choosing the right advertising method for your small business or start-up is a crucial decision.

Ideally, take time to weigh pros and cons of each of these mediums, before employing them in your next promotional activity.

1) Newspapers

You must ensure your newspaper advert is working effectively. Maintain a check list to analyse if the following are featured in your promotion.

- a) Decide on the message you are trying to express
    - Why should customers buy your product or service?
    - How can they buy it?
- b) Keep your advertisement simple and easy to read
- c) Placement is critical
    - Page 3 is the best place to advertise
    - Right hand page adverts bring in more customers
- d) Use black and white, colour or spot colours (red and blue) in your advert
- e) Size does count: The bigger the better
- f) Pay for the number of readers
    - Sunday papers have large readership
- g) Newspaper inserts
    - Have promotional brochures put inside newspapers (On Sunday papers, in particular)
- h) Make sure your advertisement stands out
    - Include quality graphics and creative work
- i) Establish credibility by using newspaper advertising
- j) Never underestimate the power of classifieds

2) Telephone Directories (Business/Residential)

a) Choosing the right directory and section are important
b) Make your advert stand out
   - Choose the right words, colours and sizes
c) Put creative ideas into your advertisement
   - Good words, photographs
d) Include big and bold questions, such as:
   - What makes us different?
   - Why should you use us?
   - Did you know?
   - Why do you think our competitors are so nervous?
   - How can we help you?
e) Don't get held up or intimidated by what your competitors are doing
f) Look at your advertisement from the customers' point of view
g) Have a strong, stand-out border
h) Have a dedicated a contact number or email to monitor responses and sales

3) Outdoor Signage

a) Roadside billboards
b) Advertisements on buses, trains, trucks, taxis
c) Signs on walls outside shopping centres, or a place where a crowd gathers
d) Advertise on bus shelters
e) Street signs
f) Signs on sporting venues
g) Outside your business venue
h) Bus or train stations

Tip: Create a message that is simple to understand, using strong and eye-catching images. Change signage regularly.

4) Direct Mail Advertising

Direct mail means advertising in the form of a direct brochure, flyer, leaflet or email to a prospective customer.

How to Make Direct Mailing Work

   a) Include correct contact details
   b) Highlight the benefits
   c) Include a statement to catch the reader's attention
   d) Offer bonus, discounts, price reduction offers
   e) Put a deadline to respond
   f) Use plain envelope
   g) Use testimonials

Why Does Direct Mailing Go Wrong?

   a) Benefits not highlighted
   b) No attention-grabbing heading
   c) Poor quality photography
   d) Poorly written
   e) Too much text, graphics, colour
   f) No discounts, or price reduction offers

5) Advertising in Magazines

   a) Magazines target a specific audience, so create your advert keeping their interests in mind.
   b) Use colours and words wisely.
   c) Advertise long term to provide a sense of credibility.
   d) Look for editorial opportunities.
   e) Include cut out coupons, discounts.
   f) Position your advert wisely.

6) Internet Advertising

   a) Give people a reason to come back.
   b) Domain name and web address are important. Having a memorable domain name is essential.

c) Banner advertising on the web needs to be bright and bold, containing minimal words.
d) Constantly review your website.
e) Animated banners are a bonus. Be careful not to make them too busy and confusing.
f) Make good use of social media networks and blogs.
g) Advertise on someone else's website or social media to attract a diverse audience and drive traffic to your website.

Tip: The real art is getting the consumer to take action after seeing your advert.

∞

Style of Writing

The first thing that attracts customers is the very bold, nicely printed first few words or sentences of an advert. Therefore, it is essential to get the customers attention before you do or say anything else.

Hence, smart phrases and opening statements are vital parts of your smart advertisement. Having your writing in a logical order for customers to better understand what you are offering differently is also important.

Incorporate these phrases, statements and styles of writing in your next advert for it to become a 'hit' in the media.

1) Phrases to Use as Headings

a) Always go to an expert...
b) Don't wait for success to come to you...
c) Go with a winner...
d) Success starts with...
e) The smart choice...

f) Turn your life around…
g) What makes us different…

2) Opening With a Question

a) Have you ever thought about…?
b) What's the best investment you could make…?
c) Why postpone your future in…?

3) Opening With a Statement

a) In today's competitive world…
b) It is never too early to…
c) It is never too late to…
d) Just a note to tell you about…
e) Today, more than ever…
f) We've got the solution to your…
g) …may determine the future of your business
h) …often spells the difference between failure and success

4) Opening With a Challenge

a) Be a winner…
b) Be your own…
c) Explore the…
d) Take a giant step…
e) …like a professional

5) Other Grabbers

a) Attention!
b) Don't miss out!
c) For a limited time only!
d) Important!
e) Valuable document(s) enclosed…

Even all of these smart writing styles are sometimes not enough to grab customers' attention in this highly competitive market.

You should also be able to think outside the box and encourage the customer to buy from you.

So, it's time to get creative and let your imagination run wild!

∞

Persuading the Customer

This is how you can persuade your customers without being too aggressive and pushing them too hard for a sale. Test these winning statements in your promotional campaigns and analyse how they can affect your sales margins and evaluate their success.

- A reward awaits you!
- Time is running out!
- You won't be disappointed!
- You'll be glad you did!
- You'll still be able to do it your way – only better!

These 'call to action' statements are also believed to influence the consumers to make that important decision to buy from you, NOW.

- Act now!
- But don't just take our word for it – find out for yourself!
- Decide for yourself!
- Don't miss this opportunity!
- It's time to make your choice!
- Make this the turning point of your life!
- Rather than simply reading about it, why don't you...?
- Take this important first step!
- Time's running out!
- You've got an important decision to make!

The following phrases are also commonly used, to create the need and desire for a potential consumer to contact the seller.

- A visit to our website is the first step
- An order form is enclosed for your convenience
- Call us this week for an appointment
- For more details, call...
- Our representative will call you at your convenience
- Please don't hesitate to call us
- Send in your application today
- We look forward to hearing from you
- Why not give us a call and find out more?
- Write for your free copy of our brochure

Finally, when your advertisement is ready to go, make sure you have a checklist to run through, and ensure your advertisement has been designed exactly the way you want it to be.

Review your advert again and again, and re-assess if you have created it in such a way to deliver the required outcomes, before it is published.

∞

The Checklist

Are you ready to launch your ad campaign? Before you do, it is important to have a check-list in place to make sure that both your advert and your message are right. Carefully consider if you have included everything you wanted just before your advert goes live.

This checklist will reduce failure due to potential errors and all these checkpoints will ensure that you have included what is necessary, and will guide you through the process of the design to keep you on track.

1) Have you checked for mistakes?
2) Colour, black and white?
3) Contact details included?
4) Have you double checked for mistakes?
5) Final call to action?

6) Logical and motivational text included?
7) Right position?
8) Right size?
9) Strong, bold heading?
10) Style of writing checked?

∞

In addition to the advertising methods already discussed, you could also use the following marketing methods to make people aware about your products and services.

Start-ups in particular, must try out all the advertising techniques they can get their hands on, until they discover the most appropriate approach for their business model.

More Advertising Practices

a) Business cards
b) Letterbox drops
c) Promotional giveaways

∞

« The Guideline »

Marketing and advertising must not only work independently, but they must work together to produce an effective outcome.

An effective marketing strategy involves smart use of colour, logos, selling methods for products and services, details of costings and time and people involved.

However, any promotional activity you are planning to use, can take time and involve hours of research if it is going to be productive.

In general, a well-planned marketing strategy must present the overall picture of how your business will be promoted and distributed, catering to the customer demands, and producing the desired outcome at the end of it.

------------ ∼∼∼∼ ------------

« CHAPTER – 8 »

Getting Your Business on the Web

The Internet represents a new frontier for commerce where an unlimited number of potential customers are just waiting to buy what you offer, online. A website is an essential marketing tool for any business and the challenge is to develop one which looks professional and easy to navigate. The moment your website goes 'live', your business becomes a global entity. And this gives small businesses the power to compete with global 'giants' in the industry.

Go Online, and Go Global!

The global accessibility and economics offered by the Internet have enabled new small and medium-sized companies to participate in the markets once reserved for only large corporations. Therefore you must not misjudge the value of getting your business on the web, which will give you the opportunity to compete with the market leaders. However, going global will bring new challenges to the business.

These are regarded as positive challenges such as the difficulty in managing volume of sales to meet demand, and management of complex distribution. However, it has already been proven that the Internet is an ideal tool for allowing businesses to compete on equal terms with much larger players.

Nevertheless, it is essential to make sure that your website looks professional and does what it is supposed to do on the Internet platform. It must clearly give customers information about your business, the services and products you offer, enabling them to contact you quickly and easily. Adding a contact form to your website for customers to make enquiries without hassle is a simple way of building an online conversation with potential buyers.

As your business expands, the amount of pages and information on the website will also increase. Therefore, it is crucial to design your website with sufficient capacity that enables you to develop with the growing traffic flow.

The designing, building and maintaining of a website involves both tangible costs such as hardware, software, equipment, etc and intangible costs such as labour, training, etc. But there's no doubt that the advantages a website can bring into a business are far greater than the costs involved. Having a well-designed website is another key factor for the growth and global expansion of your new business venture.

Therefore it is necessary to get your website set up, if you want to reach the global audience effectively. It will be especially invaluable for those who are starting out to create purposeful websites that give people a reason to get in touch.

And it is also equally important to do it 'right'. Because getting your business's online presence wrong can do more damage than good.

Hence, consider these basic initial guidelines and general rules that will help you improve your business's web-based presence.

Your website:

Rule 1: Should offer something distinctive and unique.
Rule 2: Must be simple, easy to use and fast.
Rule 3: Must be interesting enough to motivate visitors to stay for some time and return.
Rule 4: Must advertise your products and services clearly.
Rule 5: Must show contact information clearly and offer 'call-to-action' instructions for the audience, to provoke an immediate interest.

So, how do you ensure your website generates sales? This is how...

∞

A Professional Website is Essential

If you want to earn trust with potential new customers, then a professional website is one of the essential components of sealing the deal. 92% of people check a company's website before they make a purchase. It is also important to use a company email address that comes with your website name, instead of using a generic email service, which doesn't communicate a high level of professionalism to potential consumer markets.

Small businesses should think about their online presence carefully, and understand how the design of their website and email address can affect their business image worldwide. A carefully planned website will help you win business and your web presence is a vital and effective marketing tool in today's competitive market.

∞

Hire a Professional

You need to maintain your website in good order to retain customers' long-term interest. Regular updates are vital if businesses are to remain accepted. You should know by now that a good website must catch the eye and provide good content to make an impression. And the information provided on your website must also be carefully written and demonstrate attention to detail and this is skilled work.

Designing an effective website with all the 'right' features is not an easy task. Ideally you should hire a professional to design the website for you.

However, make sure that you are in agreement about the relevant terms and conditions and be aware of all the hidden costs, such as costs for regular website maintenance and updates before, handing over the design job.

Your website developer must be able to assist you with all technically related functions and maintenance as long as you need his/her services.

When there is a frequent flow of traffic, you might well need professional advice to keep the website up and running without facing any technical failures. However, it will also be helpful to take into account that there is easy to use and quick to build 'off the shelf' web designing software available in the market today. It is good enough to make use of such software to build a 'basic' website initially, when you start out. Still, it is not ideal for long term use as such websites might not be as effective as custom-built 'bespoke' websites.

∞

How to Make Your Website a Success

The widespread availability and adoption of the Internet allows consumers to directly link with your business. It should be comforting to know, as you start out, that your website is on a platform that achieves mass acceptance faster than any other technology in the market.

These days, most people will go online and do their research to learn about your business and they are most likely to find you despite their location, when you have an Internet presence. Evidently, just a simple site that tells people about your company, your products and services will be enough for your potential customer to make an initial judgment about your business.

For example, the world's largest express transportation company, takes orders from more than 200 countries around the world each business day via its website. This gives you a hint of how far you can go if your business owns a website. Small business owners in particular must advance their online presence to reach a wider market and achieve success from it.

Take the following critical success factors into consideration, when building a website that will potentially bring in more sales.

1) Research the Market

Do your research to find out who your audience and buyers would be, first. Then, tailor your website to match your market. Make sure you are targeting the correct age group and the countries where the potential customers are based. Think about the buying patterns of your customers and design the look and feel of your site according to their taste. Consider tailoring the content of your website to global standards to reach an international consumer base.

2) Use a Simple Web Domain Name

An easy to remember and simple web name is key. It is not ideal to use more than 15 characters for your web name.

Carry out checks to see if the name you have chosen is being used by anyone else, to avoid the possibility of legal action being taken against you. In the UK, Companies House is a good place to check.

It is preferable to have more than one web name in mind, in case you change your mind about the first few options.

Running brain-storming sessions with family, friends, people who support your business or focus groups to bring together ideas and decide upon the best web name will also be useful. Using a suffix such as .com or .net in your web address is important, if you are aiming to go global in the future.

3) Get the Design Right

People are more likely to visit, stay on and return to a website that looks credible. There are a number of free websites available today, as well as that you can look for a website designer whose style and clients are a good match.

Generally, simple colours, creative graphics and attention-grabbing text are fundamental to a successful website. Concise, clean and clear designs with consistent colours are important. Choosing a colour scheme to reflect products and services that you are offering is a good idea, too.

When designing the website, there are two aspects you need to think about. Firstly, an attractive graphic design, to ensure the look of the website appeals to the relevant target audience. Then, you need to use suitable font, colours and contrasts that complement each particular component as necessary.

The selection of the right font for your website and the arrangement of the wording can be hard to properly portray the mood of the website.

However, the way you are planning to use fonts within your web design is as significant as your layout or colour scheme. Furthermore, pay attention to size of the font – it needs to be easily legible and should be at least 12 point. A font style of 'serif' or 'sans serif' is compatible with most operating systems.

Make sure that you use the chosen font size and style throughout all the web pages to maintain a solid flow, except for headings and other phrases you might want to highlight (eg quotes from customers) – these might be in a larger font.

Also, think of using a sensible number of high quality images relevant to your business, while avoiding unnecessary clutter. Moreover, keep in mind that creating a unique look is vital to separate a website from its competition.

4) Never Overwrite

A crowded website with complex terms, words and images will distract people straight away. Therefore, it is most suitable to make your website as clutter-free as possible, by including just enough text and graphics to pass your message.

In this way, you will be able to create a simple and appealing brand image for your business, enabling your customers to understand the message better and quicker.

5) Keep Your Website Up to Date

Your website can be considered as the permanent online presence of your business. And you need to make sure that when people use your website, the content is up to date and easy to understand. This will increase your credibility with potential customers and they will believe that you have the latest information, and that you are aware of what is happening around you.

Business owners should bring their websites up to date every week, if relevant. Making frequent changes on the website will also improve the ranking and online visibility on search engines, which is good for any business.

6) Don't Copy and Use Others' Work Illegally

By no means use someone else's work, images, music or text which are not your own on your website.

Do your own search as to where you can get free images, or hire a reasonable photographer, or hand over the job to a creative design firm who can do the work for you.

Seven Guidelines for Exceptional Website Design

There will be no harm in taking a few extra steps to make your website considerably better. Therefore also consider the following guidelines on how you can improve the design and presentation of your company website, even further.

1) Define the Role of Your Website

This is crucial when you are thinking of developing a website. A website can be an online brochure, a tool for requesting a sales visit, or a tool to develop ongoing relationships with your consumers.

Always try to offer something unique through your website, for example, providing people with information about your products and services, which they can't find anywhere else or which are in short supply, and offering them to a global audience at a reasonable price, which will definitely lead to profitability. All business owners must ensure they have the power to do this sort of thing, through their website, to succeed.

2) Usability Design Tips

Getting the graphic design right is only the start. You also need to ensure the site is user friendly, by having a consistent structure to present information and ensuring the navigation is simple and straightforward. Websites that are easy to use, especially on mobile platforms and the latest computers and devices, are more popular these days.

It is also vital to have relevant web pages with a strong call-to-action plan. In other words, you must know what you want visitors to do next at each stage, and make that action point obvious.

3) Write Differently for the Web

People read web pages differently than they read text on paper. They speed read text about 25% faster on screen than they do on paper.

As a result, you have much less time to grab their attention and get them interested before they leave you. So, you must make sure you include shorter, sharper text and use headlines which really draw out and highlight the benefits of what your business has to offer.

Presenting a brief summary of information with hyperlinks, allowing users to 'click' only on the details they are interested in, rather than including a lot of information on a single page, is invaluable.

4) Drive Traffic to Your Site

Once the website is up and running, the next step is to promote it as necessary, such as including website details on your stationery, sales brochures, sale boards and all marketing materials, along with other contact information. Using email signatures to promote your site's web address and often highlighting new services and products on offer are smart ways of making people aware of your online presence.

Direct mail can point visitors to a specific page on your website to view a particular product or service, which will drive traffic to your website, and eventually improve your sales figures as a result.

People tend to visit websites that provide useful information, free goods and services, or discounted offers and this will be helpful to attract traffic to your website.

5) Be Friendly to Spiders and Surfers

Do not forget that there are unseen readers out there as well, who can have a significant influence on how well your website performs on search engines. Creating a website with Internet-friendly coding will rank your website at the top of search tools. However, to find out how to do this you will need to hire a professional web designer.

Also, registering your website with popular search engines such as Google and Yahoo will pull people to your business. Additionally, carry out research on other websites that allow you to advertise for free. Take advantage of every opportunity that is accessible to you.

6) Interact with Customers

Your business website must be an interactive medium that creates a dialogue with your customers. Including notice boards, discussion forums, chat windows and email options on your website will help you achieve just that. Through a subscription-based newsletter or 'notify me' facility, you will be able to create a database of potential leads effectively as well.

By going a step further, you can motivate people by creating a platform to interact with other users who share common interests. People can also exchange suggestions and ideas and post requests for you on these communication platforms, which will allow you to answer their queries quickly.

Reducing response times in this way will help you save time and build strong relationship with your consumers, which is very useful for future business growth.

7) Understand How Your Target Audience Use Your Website

Analyse your web statistics carefully and regularly, to understand how people arrive at and travel around your site.

As discussed previously, one of the most important features of your website should be to design it in such a way that your customers can easily navigate to find what they are looking for.

Assess if calls-to-action strategies on your website are working. Keep a close eye on whether people are contacting you by phone as a result of visiting your website or how many emails are coming in. Evaluate if your website has made it clear what you want people to do from each page on the site.

Take advantage of Google analytics reports, available for free, to track the behaviour of your customers on regularly, and this could provide you with important insights such as time of day and day of the week people visited, their location, number of visits achieved per day/week, most popular page of your website, etc.

These statistics are useful to make a good assessment of consumer behaviour on your website, enabling you to decide on the changes that might be necessary for improvement, and also to discover whether your website is making the expected impact on your potential customer markets or not.

Maintaining Your Website

You should always consider how you are going to engineer repeat viewings of your website, and create reasons to keep the customers coming back. The aim of an online presence is to boost sales, increase productivity, earn trust and advertise the business to a wider global audience. If you lack the knowledge to do so, it is worthwhile taking on the services of an expert.

Hence, to maintain your website in good order and allow it to deliver what is expected of it, you must consistently identify the needs for change, analyse the areas of concern for improvement, implement strategies and set up a systematic maintenance procedure. It is significantly important to make sure all the content of your website is proof read and authorised by you, or an appointed member of your team, before the changes go online.

In this digital age, the Internet has allowed businesses to break through the geographical barrier. That is why your website is a vital piece of Internet marketing, and an essential tool for branding efforts of your business.

Your website is your online store. And it is open to the world twenty four hours a day, seven days a week. Therefore never under estimate what your website can do for your business if used effectively.

« CHAPTER – 9 »

Basic Sales Techniques

Traditional sales activities involve cost-intensive and labour intensive face-to-face meetings, phone calls and business trips. Today, as a result of various types of free and cost effective Internet based sales techniques, the costly and timely sales tasks have been greatly reduced.

Moreover, there are numerous effective strategies, models and methods that have been developed for businesses to help make sales in a more productive manner.

One such model commonly used by sales teams today (and mentioned in Chapter 7) is AIDA.

For anyone starting out in their small business journey and getting ready to make a sale, it is important to take into account the following fundamental steps explained in the marketing communication tool AIDA to achieve the best outcome.

- ♦ A – Catch the customer's **Attention**
- ♦ I – Generate the customer's **Interest**
- ♦ D – Establish the customer's **Desire** to buy
- ♦ A – Confirm the **Actions to be** taken

Before making a sale, it is vital to create a good impression on your potential customer, about both you and your business. Building trust is 'key' for a successful sale.

This is what you should do to prepare yourself for a great sales pitch, and prepare yourself to 'talk the talk'.

a) Do your research well in advance.
b) Prevent marketing materials from going to waste. Be creative with the message you are planning to put across.
c) Gain potential customers' attention with a good design or a statement that creates an immediate interest.
d) Explain the benefits of your product or service clearly.
e) Explain the benefits to create the desire to buy.
f) Include a 'call to action' or offer discounts.
g) Mention the benefits of an after sales service, if available.

It is very important to incorporate your contact details such as telephone number, email address, business address and website details on all your advertisements and marketing materials. At the end of every sales conversation, reiterate what has been agreed and confirm the next steps.

Finally, send a confirmation email, text or letter to close the deal.

In Summary, every stage of the 'sale cycle' from initiating to closing a deal must be supported with information transparent to both the seller and buyer.

Furthermore, every sales activity must be monitored to ensure that consumers are being offered great services, which will earn their trust and build a strong long term-relationship.

∞

Sales Interface

The sales interface of any business in general consists of five main units that work together: finance, marketing, customers, competition and sales.

Customer needs
+
Customer satisfaction

Sales Interface

As a business owner it is vital to always ensure that you are able to maintain a good communication channel to improve and develop a good business relationship with all these entities that are in charge of various functions within the business's sales interface.

Each and every entity is directly inter-linked on the sales platform. This means that if one association is damaged then there's a high risk of the whole sales process being jeopardised.

Therefore, the presence of these elements, their inputs and their accurate maintenance within the business boundary, are all required to improve the company's productivity, to avoid clashes and to avoid failure in the overall business operation.

Being aware of how and when to employ these entities efficiently is crucial for the future progression of the business. Therefore, keeping a careful eye on every unit is essential.

The 'Sales Interface' indicates how essential it is to maintain an efficient relationship among the important entities of your business, your team and your customers and for them to interact with each other effectively, in order to progress to the next level successfully.

∞

Customer-Oriented Selling

All your business and sales must be based on customer needs and preferences. If there are no customers, there are no sales.

Always remember that the customer is the 'key' to your business success. Therefore, all your decisions must be made keeping their interests in mind. And it is worthwhile taking the following hints and tips into account when making a sale.

As stated before, you must:

- Assess your customers' needs first
- Offer products and services that will satisfy those needs
- Offer alternative products and services, if available
- Help your customers to make the best purchasing decision
- Never force your customers to make the purchase. Allow them sufficient time to make up their minds

Talk to Your Customers

When you speak to your customers your primary focus should be to offer your 'best' deal to them. Knowing what they want early on will help you plan for the sale better.

When meeting your customers face-to-face, note down what their exact requirements are so that you can, provide the best service or product available. Earning the customer's trust and showing you care will most certainly seal the deal.

It is worth taking notes of each conversation you have had, and saving email communications, and referring to them before making the 'follow up call' to potential buyers.

Educating your sales team on the most effective sales techniques is essential for progression of the business. Training your team to follow the guidelines below will certainly help you achieve your sales targets and more.

a) Learn to listen – Often the best sales people are those who listen more than they talk. Paying attention to the customer's needs makes them feel important.

b) Ask the right opening questions – Always start with questions that can only be answered with 'Yes'.

c) Move on to open-ended questions – This will reveal more about their needs.

d) Ask the customer if they have any query, doubt or difficulty regarding your product or service.

e) After a customer makes a purchase or pays a visit, ensure that you send a text or an email to say 'thank you'.

Types of Customers

There are different categories of customers in the market. Therefore, it is significantly important to have a good understanding of your target market and the type of customers your products and services appeal to.

Also, recognising the characteristics of the customer you are dealing with from the beginning will help you plan the sales strategies easily. Knowing the most common types of customers that exist in the market in general and learning the differences in their personalities will undoubtedly help you in planning your marketing strategies effectively.

1) **Enthusiast** – This type loves a conversation. Therefore, sales people can talk to them as much as they like. Listen to them carefully, answer all their queries and doubts, explain in detail, spend time with them, and they will be most likely to make a purchase from you.

2) **Considerate** – Compassionate. Therefore, it is easier for a salesperson to persuade them to make a purchase. However, do not take advantage of their caring nature and rush them into a sale. Be honest to establish a long-term relationship with them.

3) **Conservative** – This type of customer loves to talk about facts, figures, numbers and data. They are more likely to get detailed facts and carry out research before they make a purchase. Therefore don't expect to have long conversations with them. However, be well prepared and give them precise and logical information when requested.

4) **Hard Bargainer** – Difficult people to deal with. If you cannot match their price, say NO. Recognising this type early will help you save energy and time for another business task, or to sell to another customer.

5) **Stable** – Sales people need to earn trust from this type of customer, as they are steady and predictable. You might need to spend time with them providing facts and figures. The selling process will be long. Give them time to think and decide. Don't force a sale with them. But persevere, as these customers will be most likely to buy from you.

6) **Driver** – Be quick and brief with this type of customer. Talk less about your products and services. But attempt to bring value to them fast, and they will be inclined to buy from you.

7) **Straight Shooter** – This type is the most honest, quite blunt or frank. Earn their trust, build long-term relationships and they will buy from you and stick with you for as long as they can.

By knowing these buyers and customer types when you are preparing for a sale, you are more likely to improve your chances of increasing your sales figures.

Keep the well-known phrase, 'information is KING' in mind; it is your responsibility as a business owner to make as much information as is appropriate and relevant available to your customers, if you intend to become a market leader.

∞

Motivational Schemes

There are many different ways to increase customer motivation and create an interest in buying from you.

Motivating people to buy from you is important. However, it is never a good idea to try to manipulate your customers into buying something from you that doesn't satisfy their needs. If you do so, people will not stick with you for long and you will also risk losing your credibility.

The following are a few suggestions to impress your potential consumers and encourage them to keep buying from you:

- Thank them for giving you their custom
- Invitation to participate in special offers/new product launching events
- Offering a coffee or drink when the customers visit you
- Sending personalised greetings for birthdays and special occasions
- Sending seasonal greetings
- Valuing their feedback regularly

However, appropriate motivational strategies within your business must be carried out with genuine and honest intentions in mind.

∞

10 Secrets of a Successful Salesperson

Generally, successful sales people have a high level of optimism and they are masters of psychology. Knowing how to be a good salesman is priceless. Your sales team must take the time to study the art of selling and they must be trained to apply best practices in their daily routine to be successful.

Do small things that will stick in your customers' minds such as a sincere and honest 'thank you'. And ensure your customers are treated as your most important asset. The way you interact with your customer will be a key factor in whether the customer will return or not.

A good sales-person must be confident and exhibit several different characteristics to be able to make a great sale and ensure that your customers return.

Remember, when you are hiring salespeople you are hiring the future of your company.

In general, 'top' salespeople are known to possess these ten valuable characteristics. Hence, as a business owner it would be ideal to look for people like this, and put together a great sales team to realise growth in your sales margins.

1) Attention to detail
2) Compassionate
3) Doing more than paid for
4) Enthusiastic
5) Good decision maker
6) Pleasing personality
7) Positive attitude
8) Responsible
9) Self-controlled
10) Unwavering

Skills of a Salesperson

Tip: Sales Performance = Ability x Motivation

This formula shows that, a top sales performance is due to the ability of a motivated sales-person. A great sales-person is believed to have the following fundamental skills:

- Fast learning
- Good communication
- Good presentation
- Research

Successful Sales Presentations

A sales presentation is a great chance for entrepreneurs to introduce their business and its benefits to potential buyers.

The key to delivering an effective sales pitch is in the preparation.

These tips apply regardless of what you are selling, where you are selling, when you are selling or to whom you are selling. Therefore, preparing for a sales pitch with these essential tips in mind will be helpful to increase your chances of winning new deals.

a) **Organise** what you want to say in your presentation into sections for easy reference, and build up a logical order that will help your potential customers to better understand your products or services.

b) **Find facts and figures** that support your argument, such as similar businesses that have already benefited from your product or service.

c) **The Message** – Make sure your audience will remember what you present. Always focus on the needs of the customer. Most people recall clearly what is said at the beginning and end of a presentation.

Therefore, build your key points into these sections. Work out the message you want to express, and make sure you have hand-outs of all the important information or the key messages you want to put across.

d) **Think about any doubts** the audience might have, and prepare your responses well in advance, as part of the presentation. Do not panic. Be honest about your answers, and execute your presentation as planned, and all will fall into place as expected.

e) **Avoid asking anyone to hold on or wait** for you to find out something, as most people will not be happy to do this. Also, your audience expect you to know your product or service reasonably well. Hence good preparation is required.

f) Make sure you **know the products and services** that your direct competitors offer, and be ready to answer any questions that may be asked.

g) **Give out promotional material** – At the end of the presentation, make sure that you have promotional material available for the audience, with your contact details included.

h) **Next Step** – Once you have dealt with any queries raised by the audience, find out if they want to arrange to place an order or have another meeting or if they need further information. Organise 'follow-up' meetings sooner rather than later, before people forget you or their interest fades.

These simple guidelines will help you engage your audience more effectively and ultimately make the way for a sale or two, or more.

> *Tip: It is extremely important to be confident about what you are selling, and make sure that your customers have a genuine need for your service or product.*

∞

Negotiating a Sale

Here are some guidelines for you to consider once you have gained the attention and trust of your customer and you believe that there is a chance of a sale.

- By now you should already know that it is of paramount importance that you understand the customer's needs. Therefore, asking questions to find out as much as you can about their exact needs, alternatives and budget are essential.
- Decide how important the deal is. Think about if it could bring in more business or boost your cash flow, while keeping your customer's interests in mind.
- Listen carefully to what the customer is saying. Note down details if necessary, and clarify details with them.

- Set out your objectives and decide which are negotiable.
- Ask for a break if you need time to think.
- Give other cost effective options, if necessary.
- Show testimonials and customer satisfaction surveys, if required.
- Allow customers time to think.
- Summarise the decisions you have reached. And let the customer know your decision as soon as you can.

Furthermore, you need to completely avoid the following; if you don't, you will risk losing a potential consumer too early.

- Don't be forceful. If it is too obvious that you need the deal, the price may get pushed down, or the customer may leave you completely.
- Don't compromise too easily.
- Never give unnecessary discounts. If you do, other customers may find out and may not trust you in the future.
- Don't make last-minute decisions, unless the decision you are about to take, is worth the risk.
- Don't give away too much. If someone has agreed to buy, don't throw in extras for free.
- Never promise what you cannot deliver. This will only damage your relationship and reputation.

If you and your sales team can stick to these general rules of sales success, then there's no doubt that your next sales pitch will be a rewarding one.

∞

Selling Styles

There are distinct selling styles employed by professional sales people. Failure to use and understand these styles can cause lost sales and frustration, especially for new businesses.

Therefore, it goes without saying how important it can be for entrepreneurs to learn what selling style or combination of styles suits their business the best. This is because the selling style you employ within your sales interface may ultimately determine your overall business success.

Consequently, it would be an added advantage for everyone who owns a business to be well aware of these selling styles as early as possible in their business journey.

a) **'The Closer' Style** – Sells not only the product, but also the complete package and the concept. This type of selling is most suitable for products and services with little or no direct competition. This will be most appropriate for new products and services that have never been invented before or are not very common in the market.

b) **'The Builder' Style** – This is all about entrepreneurial spirit of sales. This is the backbone of most businesses, as this sells well accepted products or services that take a long-term approach. However, this adds value through creative problem solving, attention to detail and ensuring reliable delivery.

c) **'The Captain and Crew' Style** – Associated with retail sales. This offers low price and maximum convenience to the customer. However, the success of this selling style completely relies upon strong sales management leadership and an empowered sales force.

d) **'Push and Pull' style** – 'Push' is used when the salesperson literally pushes the idea of buying the product or service on the buyer. 'Pull' is when a situation is created where the seller, through skilful questioning and understanding of the needs of the buyer, nudges him/her towards a decision. This is generally considered as a 'smart' way of selling. However, you must ensure not to push a potential too hard when you are trying to make a sale.

e) **'The Wizard' Style** – This sells high tech products or services that are customised to meet an organisations' requirements. This is all about creating unique solutions.

Therefore, anyone running a business of their own should empower themselves with the understanding of these basic sales techniques and watch the sales take off.

Learn what really works for you and always remember that selling is easy when you work hard at it.

> *Tip: Practice your selling skills and techniques. Never forget the rule 'Practice makes perfect!. Make your next sale better. Build confidence. Offer an honest service to your customer.*

« CHAPTER – 10 »

Using the Latest Technology in Your Business

Information Technology (IT) is no longer a business resource, it has become the business environment on which the most of today's businesses depend. IT helps you run your business in a more efficient and effective way eliminating or minimising human errors.

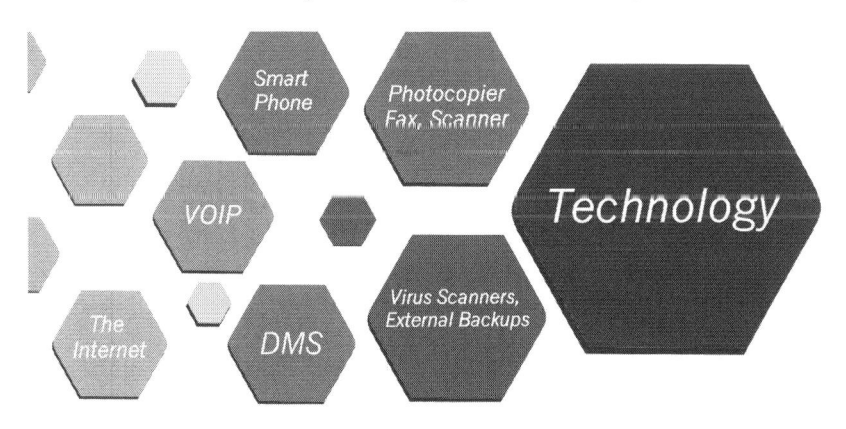

Using the Latest Technology in Your Business

Incorporating the above innovative technologies in a business venture will enable it to increase its chances of growing into a flourishing future market leader.

Currently in the world of business, use of latest innovative technology has become the core means to improve sales and growth. However, business owners must find the right business technologies relevant to their needs to reap the best benefits that IT has to offer. It is important that computers and the other latest tech gadgets of innovative technology are used in the right way to maximise productivity and realise true business success.

It is a well-known fact that business owners who use technology have a competitive advantage over similar businesses in the market.

The Internet

In the 21st century, it is increasingly difficult to imagine how businesses can be conducted without the Internet. The Internet has become a 'must have' for all types of businesses, irrespective of their size and type. The Internet has transformed people's lives and revolutionised the way people do business at both a local and global level.

The Internet has brought the world considerably closer, enabling business organisations to reach a diverse consumer base. This is extremely useful, especially if you are a small business competing with larger rivals.

The Internet can decrease overhead costs, which is one of the key fundamentals that can help you grow your business in today's competitive economy.

As many businesses rely heavily on the Internet for all aspects of their business operation today, effective use of broadband in relevant areas will enable a business to have a fast Internet connection and respond to consumers much quicker. Also, efficient use of the Internet can greatly reduce travel cost and time.

When modern businesses depend heavily on the Internet it may add additional pressure as well, in terms of protection and precautions related to data security. Therefore, if you are a frequent user of the Internet it is important to get relevant security features such as virus scanners added to your website, email platforms, databases, etc to protect your data from online intruders. Making sure that you purchase the latest version of software and update your equipment periodically is crucial to the undisrupted operation of your business.

Considering the above alone, the benefits the Internet can bring into your business are far greater than its drawbacks. And it is essential that you make use of effective Internet facilities if you are planning to build a successful enterprise in the near future.

VoIP

Many companies use VoIP (Voice over Internet Protocol) as their main communication channel. This is a cost effective way of communicating and discussing important deals, business matters, having meetings and sharing files and documents with business partners, co-workers, clients and customers across the world. Use of Skype is a common example of such a communication tool.

Video conferencing is also one of the facilities that has been incorporated into VoIP technology and is already a popular method of communication among local and global business ventures.

Using a VoIP system has several benefits for both a business and its consumers, such as cutting down telecommunication costs considerably, eliminating costly long-distance traditional calls and saving travel time.

Therefore, IT gurus believe use of such effective methods of communication plays a very important role in any type and size of business in today's market.

Document Management Systems (DMS)

As your business begins to grow the number of documents that has to be stored, referred to and used also increases. Storing such documents in a storage unit, cupboard or file in your business premises or home is not secure enough, in case a disaster such as fire, flood strikes or theft happens.

Therefore, implementing a DMS will enable you to enhance security and improve control mechanism of all your business functions, by keeping all your important business documents, financial data and marketing materials safe on a computer-based system. Managing documents in an orderly manner in your computer or on an internal disk or external disk will save you time as well, when locating documents at busy times.

Making sure that you have enough memory space in your computer or internal/external disks/cloud space to be able to handle the work load is also vital, while keeping them securely. External hard drives or storage systems such as Internet cloud are available if you do not have sufficient memory space on your computers.

It is also important to create data back-up at regular intervals to eliminate the risk of losing valuable business information. Being certain that all your important documents are backed up, safe from viruses and stored in a safe place is a relief for any business owner.

Virus Scanners and External Backup

Installing a reliable virus scanner on your computers will keep you safe from threats, infections and viruses. However, you must also remember that virus scanners will not always protect your computer.

Therefore, it is essential to be vigilant about suspicious emails that you might receive and malicious software that might harm your computer system.

Keeping external backup of your important data in a remote location will also protect your information from loss as a result of floods, fire or theft.

Photocopier, Fax and Scanner

These items of office equipment are 'must have's' if you are running a business irrespective of the business location, whether you are operating from home or a city office.

It would be very useful to have a photocopier, fax or scanner installed even when your business operations are minimal.

All parties in the business interface, such as your suppliers, customers, marketing team, distributors and even your accountant, should be able to reach you and share documents and information with you quickly and easily, twenty four hours a day and seven days a week.

Your business must be able to run as efficiently as possible to gain the highest productivity. Using this equipment appropriately will definitely help you to achieve this aim.

Smart phone

This is an era of smart-phones. The majority of your potential customers can be found using smart-phones nowadays.

Therefore, it is necessary to ensure your website, software and applications are smart-phone compatible to get the best out of them.

Moreover, there's a great tendency for people to shop online in the current economic climate.

And you must observe the shifting buying patterns and behaviours, use the latest devices, be up to date and change as the market changes, if you are to stay ahead and in fact 'do better' than your competition.

∞

Information System Benefits

The primary benefit of information systems is their ability to provide a business with the information needed to perform any task effectively. Combining the use of information systems and the latest technology can enable a business to streamline its entire operations into a cohesive unit that will contribute to increased productivity and improved competence in the long run. Here's how your overall business operation will be benefited by the appropriate use of innovative technologies and information systems.

- Better control of finance and resources
- Better management and increased staff morale
- Enhanced competitive advantage
- Improved business functions and innovative strategies
- Improved communication
  Improved customer service
- Increased product quality and reliability
- Shorter development time leading to lower costs

However, to implement advanced systems in a business one must clearly understand how, when and where such systems could be applied to reap the best rewards. And there's no doubt that by adding these systems into your business model you will be able to achieve the highest productivity and a better outcome.

∞

Porter's Five Forces Model

This is a well-recognised business model and its concept has been used by many successful businesses around the world. Porter's strategies describe how a company can pursue competitive advantage across its chosen market, by concentrating on its external threats and understanding their nature.

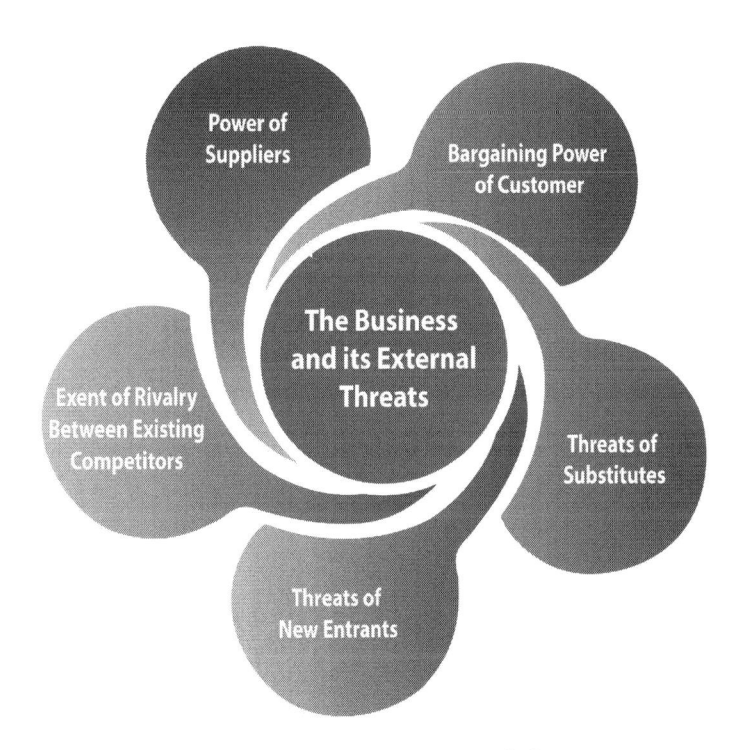

Porter's Five Forces Model

This commonly used business model includes tips on how to apply each strategy within your business which will direct you towards a much secure and steady future.

The five forces, power of customers, power of suppliers, threats of substitutes, threats of new entrants, and rivalry between competitors that would impact an organisation's behaviour in a competitive market, must be identified from the very early days of any business.

Porter's generic strategies help you compete effectively with your rivals no matter what industry you are in. This business model identifies the external forces that will affect an organisation and helps you evaluate how the company can stay in shape and how such information can be used to positively respond to them without being severely affected.

Knowing the threats you are likely to face and your capabilities and powers to stand firm against them, you will enable you to keep your business intact.

Once these external threats have been correctly recognised, your company is able to apply its core competencies to reduce the effects of the 'five forces' and perform better to stand out in the market you operate in.

∞

Competitive Strategies

A business's position within its industry is determined by its profitability and brand image.

Nearly 80% of business owners believe the quality of a service or product is the fundamental means of achieving competitive advantage. A long-term action plan is required to help a company gain this competitive advantage over its rivals.

Decisions generate action that produces results. These results are the consequences of the decisions made. Often, entrepreneurs are faced with situations in which quick strategic decisions are required to secure the business's foreseeable future.

Hence, it is necessary for organisations to adopt good leadership strategies focusing on differentiation and use of innovation to continually grow. Such strategies should be designed and the decision should be taken with clear vision, mission and policies and good use of competitive forces in mind.

A company will be able to maintain its competitive advantage based on efficient use of these competitive forces. Through an effective combination of knowledge and technology you must aim to:

- Achieve lower costs
- Build a well-known brand and reputation

- Create the best products and services on the market
- Deliver the best customer service
- Provide the best value for money

While achieving the above, an organisation's strategy can also be rooted in four areas:

1) Vision
2) Mission
3) Strategies
4) Policies

Therefore, entrepreneurs have to create their own road-map of business. And their primary aim must be to develop strategies that will help them gain an insight into future opportunities and plan to utilise those strategies in the best possible way. It is never a good idea to target competitors' products or services by reproducing their features; rather, you should attempt to make your products or services unique.

∞

Use of Project Management Software

Every growing business has different project plans in place for further development. These development activities involve planning, organising and control of resources, procedures and rules to achieve specific goals.

To plan and execute these projects accurately, the people involved must apply their knowledge, skills and practices appropriately in order to succeed.

As previously mentioned, there is a variety of management software available in the market today, at a cost effective price, which has the capacity to help you manage these projects easily.

Such project management software will offer you varied features to plan, control and manage resources easily and effectively for further development and growth.

∞

Activities Involved in a Project

Whether you are planning to launch a new product/service, improve existing products/services, or arrange the next marketing activity in your business, you must have a clear vision of what your goals are and when you are expecting to achieve them.

Therefore, any projects involving a plan for growth must be carefully considered. The following guidelines will assist you to do just that.

1) **Business Objectives and Requirements** – When initiating a new project plan, a company must check if the proposed system is aligned with the current business needs. If not, the project will not be constructive and effective for the purpose.

2) **Feasibility and Responsibilities** – This is the most important aspect of the initial project plan. A cost-benefit analysis must be performed to assess if the proposed project is feasible and produces expected positive results.

   In addition, it is necessary to define the exact roles and responsibilities for managers, staff and users, for this new system to function productively.

3) **Identify Constraints** – Recognising the limitations of a project and establishing budget and timescale are necessary here. Producing an approximate estimation of project size and complexity should also be detailed clearly on the initial project plan. This will be helpful for the management and developers to decide if the entire project strategy is a viable one.

4) **Scope** – The scope of the project must be to carefully consider and involve boundaries, which describe the parts of the business that will be affected by implementing new the system. Carry out an investigation to find out whether this project is worth developing or not.

5) **Risks** – It is essential to identify potential problems and risks early, which may cause the projects to fail. This can include shortage of skills, changes in the market, financial difficulties, etc. Therefore, a necessary precaution plan must be integrated to prevent or eliminate those risk factors.

Final points to bear in mind...

∞

Why Do Projects Fail?

In general, business owners have various project plans prepared for further improvement. However, often these project plans can fail at any stage of the business. So, it is essential for anyone running a business to have a reasonable knowledge of why and how such projects fail.

How do you know when and why a project has failed? In many cases, the reason for failure is obvious. Generally, every failed project will have its own set of errors. Therefore, it is important for entrepreneurs to understand the main reasons for such failures.

Out of many reasons, the most common would be:

a) Failures in internal organisational structure
b) Failures of users/staff
c) Failures in the business environment: The background of the business may change or does not exist anymore
d) Technical issues

However, to minimise the above, business owners must focus on the following fundamental project management tips, and have a backup plan or two ready to avoid the potential collapse of overall business functions.

- Accurate project documentation
- An accurate schedule with a well-planned set of tasks
- An estimate of costs, times and resources
- Implementation of a good system to monitor and control project performance

When you are planning a project, you must recognise the objectives of the project and goals that you are hoping to achieve at the end of it.

And every project must have three key features. The **scope**, which is what your project is trying to accomplish and what unique service or product is expected as a result, **time** and **cost**.

Hence, it is essential for entrepreneurs to be aware of each and every task involved in a project to ultimately achieve success.

Project Goals

One must thoroughly understand what needs to be done to identify familiar indicators and warning signs of a project in trouble, early on. Great leaders will pay attention to the following, to achieve project goals effectively and successfully.

1) Avoid budget overruns to stay within the budget
2) Avoid quality flaws to meet the specified quality
3) Avoid schedule slippage to deliver on schedule
4) Deliver the expected end-products

Behind every successful project, there is an insightful project manager who:

- Embraces change
- Encourages new ideas

- Has great leadership skills
- Is a good communicator and negotiator
- Is technically competent

Therefore, business owners must not forget the importance of employing the right people on the right projects who have the right skills and attitude to achieve a winning end result with their project goals.

∞

Outsourcing

Outsourcing is the allocation of business tasks to a third-party or an outside company, which is considered as an effective cost-saving strategy when used correctly. Outsourcing can offer companies an essential strategy and leadership across shared sourcing.

Sometimes it is ideal for a business to outsource some of its tasks to professionals or a third party when there is a lack of skills, resources, and infrastructure or there are functions that are difficult to manage. By outsourcing, businesses are able to produce the best products and services possible and achieve the highest productivity. Opting to outsource will also allow you to focus on mission-critical activities and organise the resources in the most efficient manner.

However, outsourcing does have its drawbacks too. Therefore, businesses must identify pros and cons to outsourcing, and decide on the areas that could have the potential for outsourcing opportunities. Yet, the decision to outsource is a crucial one. And you must carry out appropriate research and preparation to recognise the need for outsourcing and avoid making a serious business mistake.

Furthermore, it is also important to evaluate potential outsourcing partners and choose the 'best fit' for the company in terms of their expertise and experience to get the best out of them and to achieve a greater outcome.

Outsourcing can generate the following positive outcomes such as:

1) General cost savings and reduction on operating costs
2) Improved service quality
3) Ability to access and apply expertise knowledge

These will result in improved efficiency, which is essential for a business to capture the market.

Businesses that outsource can achieve this with the minimal capital investment and the highest expert service.

4) Ability to access best facilities and resources
5) Improved scalability

By being able to extend your business activities you will be able to handle large volumes of business activities faster which would be important for a new business to grow rapidly.

The important fact is that outsourcing will enable you to achieve this, using a third party's robust infrastructure and enhanced scalability.

6) Improved company focus and motivation
7) Free management time to pay attention to other tasks
8) Reduction of risks and threats

When there are too many things to handle, this can detract from focusing on a business's core activities. When that happens, things can clearly go out of control. Therefore, if outsourced appropriately, your company will have sufficient time to better focus on the core competencies and objectives.

9) Additional cash infusion and more capital funds available
10) Improved financial control and availability of funds for other areas and tasks

Often, businesses can seriously jeopardise customer relationships and overall customer satisfaction by taking a long time over business development activities.

In addition, performing in-house expansion strategies is extremely expensive and time consuming. Once those strategies have been implemented, businesses take time to adapt to these changes, too.

Therefore, taking the above benefits into account, outsourcing can be regarded as the best solution to the above circumstances.

Two further benefits of outsourcing are:

11) More free resources
12) Increased flexibility

By considering all these advantages of outsourcing, it would appear that the concept of contracting out selected tasks can provide invaluable growth opportunities for small and medium businesses in particular.

Even though outsourcing can enable you to capitalise on your core efficiencies, you need to do your research as necessary to choose the right outsource partner to gain the maximum yield for your business.

Nevertheless, there are also some common and distinct disadvantages to outsourcing, among them the loss of control of some of the business functions. Regardless of whom you outsource to, you are still responsible for the quality of what you produce while maintaining satisfactory customer relationships.

Therefore, you must clearly understand and evaluate the risks and benefits of outsourcing, before committing to it.

Evaluating Potential Outsourcing Partners

Clearly, you need to be careful when choosing your outsourcing partner.

Once you have decided to outsource, you must cautiously monitor the procedures and performance of the partner, otherwise you will risk permanently pushing away the customers you have worked so hard to attract.

The key to a successful outsourcing partnership relies on understanding the whole process, specifying objectives clearly, establishing internal and external company procedures, evaluation of performance against objectives, and deploying a transparent system that helps manage and supervise all the functionalities involved.

Additionally, both parties must be aware of the applicable local tax regulations to avoid complications arising.

Tip: Outsourcing is the way forward.

The following tips will help you, administer the outsourcing process and still maintain a good relationship with both your outsourcing partners and customers.

- Establish a measurable system to evaluate and review performance
- Monitor customer feedback and satisfaction levels
- As sales volumes grow, re-evaluate decisions on outsourced tasks
- Maintain a strong communication channel with outsourcing partners and your customer base

Also, if something goes wrong, all the parties should discuss it, and do what is necessary to correct the situation as quickly as possible. Companies nowadays are increasingly embracing outsourcing across a wider range of business functions to help them develop their businesses rapidly.

Therefore, it is recommended for new business owners to integrate proven practices of outsourcing in suitable areas to drive business growth and innovation.

If you are a serious business looking to experience effective cost-saving strategies, then careful use of outsourcing plans in your business could be a lifesaver.

Embracing outsourcing enthusiastically rather than ignoring the concept completely is the way forward, especially if you are thinking of accelerating the development of your small/medium business's future.

« AUTHOR'S NOTE »

As you are making the challenging decision to set up your own business, knowing that the direction towards success will be a bumpy road can be an overwhelming thought. However, knowing the rules and boundaries, your limitations and abilities, and when to stop early, will save you from many pitfalls along the way.

I genuinely hope that this book has given you some important secrets, ideas, tips and step-by-step guidance on how to get started on your business journey. And I hope the information will prove invaluable as you are starting out.

It is time to do something you love and become your own BOSS by creating a business of your own.

Initially, the path to success might be a lonely one. And never assume that the road ahead is just like the road behind.

Persevere! Gear up for the challenging journey ahead!

GOOD LUCK!

REFERENCES

Michael E. Porter. "The Five Competitive Forces that Shape Strategy", Harvard Business Review, January 2008, p.86-104